Team Investigation of Child Sexual Abuse

Interpersonal Violence:
The Practice Series
Jon R. Conte, Series Editor

Interpersonal Violence: The Practice Series is devoted to mental health, social service, and allied professionals who confront daily the problem of interpersonal violence. It is hoped that the knowledge, professional experience, and high standards of practice offered by the authors of these volumes may lead to the end of interpersonal violence.

In this series...

Team Investigation of Child Sexual Abuse

The Uneasy Alliance

Donna Pence
Charles Wilson

Interpersonal Violence:
The Practice Series

SAGE Publications
International Educational and Professional Publisher
Thousand Oaks London New Delhi

For information address:

SAGE Publications, Inc.
2455 Teller Road
Thousand Oaks, California 91320
E-mail: order@sagepub.com

SAGE Publications Ltd.
6 Bonhill Street
London EC2A 4PU
United Kingdom

SAGE Publications India Pvt. Ltd.
M-32 Market
Greater Kailash I
New Delhi 110 048 India

Printed in the United States of America

Library of Congress Cataloging-in-Publication Data

Pence, Donna.
    Team investigation of child sexual abuse: the uneasy alliance/
authors Donna Pence, Charles Wilson.
        p.   cm. — (Interpersonal violence: The practice series; v.
6)
    Includes bibliographical references and index.
    ISBN 0-8039-5169-8 (cloth). — ISBN 0-8039-5170-1 (pbk.)
    1. Child sexual abuse—Investigation.   2. Work groups.
I. Wilson, Charles (Charles Albert)   II. Title.   III. Series:
Interpersonal violence: The practice series; v. 6.
HV8079.C48P46   1994
363.2 ' 59536—dc20   94-28880

96 97 98 99 00 01 10 9 8 7 6 5 4 3 2

Sage Production Editor: Yvonne Könneker

Contents

Acknowledgments

We wish to acknowledge the host of colleagues whose insights, experiences, research, and inspiration contributed to this work. Of special note are those within the Tennessee Bureau of Investigation, the Tennessee Department of Human Services, and the Tennessee Child Sexual Abuse Task Force, as well as the American Professional Society on the Abuse of Children, the Tennessee Network on Child Advocacy, and the Tennessee Professional Society on the Abuse of Children. Individuals who have personally influenced our work and thinking and deserve special acknowledgement include Joe and Laurie Braga, John Briere and Cheryl Langtree, Kee MacFarlane and Harry Elias, Jim Paavola, Bill Murphy, Susan Steppe, Lucy Berliner, Theresa Reid, Barbara Bonner, Jim Pryor, Kathleen Faller, John Meyers, Patty Toth, Paul Stern, Bonnie Benke, Terry Hazard, Ethel Amacher, David Finkelhor, Roland Summitt, Linda Williams, Susan Kelly, Joyce Thomas, Mark Everson, and Anna Salter. We also wish to acknowledge the original Child Protective Investigative Team in Dyer County, Tennessee, which served as a laboratory for new ideas more than a decade ago and started it all for us; Bill Covington, who helped pass the law that forced our introduction; and the hundreds of team members across the nation with whom we have met and who have invited us into their communities to train and learn from their experiences. A special note of appreciation goes to our reviewers— David Chadwick and Ken Lanning—and to our editor and friend, Jon Conte.

On a personal note, we must express our appreciation to Judith Brown for her editorial assistance and Mary Tidwell for her impromptu word-processing lessons and guidance. Finally, to our children: Krista for her patience as we traveled far and wide, and Alexis and Lucy for their uninformed consent to be small child-development laboratories for us as we marveled at the stages of cognitive and language development as they passed through them on life's journey. This work is dedicated to them and to all children. May we find a way to stop the hurt forever.

1

Introduction: The Team Investigation of Child Sexual Abuse

What is known about child sexual assault has undergone profound changes since 1980. Correspondingly, in many communities the system that will respond to reports of child sexual abuse in the mid-1990s will bear little resemblance to the intervention system of 1980. Through the integration of practical experience, enhanced statutory frameworks, case law, and research, professionals working in sexual abuse cases may well be more skillful, make better decisions, and do so in a way that is less traumatic for the children involved.

❑ Growth in Reporting

Until the 1980s, child sexual abuse was a minor part of the caseload of child protection agencies and even a smaller part of the lives of law enforcement officers. Reports of this form of child maltreatment represented only 7% of the 850,000 child abuse and neglect referrals received across the nation in 1981 (American Humane Association, 1983). Although statistics on criminal investigations or prosecutions on child sexual assault in the 1970s or before are not available, there is ample reason to believe that such events were comparatively rare. Below the surface of public and professional awareness, however, was a vast reservoir of children in need of protection.

Researchers have documented the prevalence of the crime of sexual abuse of children for many years. As early as the 1950s, Landis was reporting that 35% of women had been sexually assaulted as minors (Landis, 1956). In more recent years, researchers have found between 27% (Finkelhor & Hotaling, 1989) and 38% (Russell, 1983) of women report childhood sexual victimization. Prevalence figures for males are more recent in origin. One commonly quoted figure for male victimization is 16% (Finkelhor & Hotaling, 1989). Although such figures are of interest to academics, they also are important to law enforcement and child protection professionals. Anecdotal evidence suggests that child sexual abuse is perhaps the most common serious criminal act involving children in our society. If we believe children are entitled to the protection of society so that they may grow up free of sexual victimization, then we must take this crime seriously.

Child sexual abuse is perhaps the most common serious criminal act involving children in our society.

With so many victims in society, it is not surprising that, with the dramatic expansion of media attention and growing public awareness, reports to law enforcement and child protection agencies have skyrocketed. Throughout the 1980s, referrals of sexual abuse climbed steadily. By 1991, nearly 2.7 million reports of child abuse and neglect (of all types) were received (National Committee on the Prevention of Child Abuse, 1992), with sexual abuse accounting for 15% (more than 400,000). This rapid expansion in reports has stretched available investigative resources, sometimes beyond the breaking point.

In many places in this country, allegations of child abuse are not being investigated by some of the very agencies designated to protect children and investigate crime. Even when all investigating agencies initiate action, they may do so in an uncoordinated manner. The result is inefficient use of resources and less-than-accurate investigations.

The cost of failure in this field can be enormous. On the one hand, a misjudgment in the investigative phase can incorrectly label an innocent party as a child molester and bring all of the adverse consequences associated with it. On the other hand, an inaccurate investigative finding can, and probably often does, mean continued sexual abuse for a child, abuse that at times is mixed with serious physical abuse and which can be fatal. Errors also can mean that the abuser remains free to prey on others.

Those who abuse children sexually do not fit any neat profile or pattern (Finkelhor, 1984). There are individuals who may only fantasize about sexual interaction with minors in much the same way a married person might fantasize about a sexual contact with someone other than his or her spouse without ever acting on it. Investigators will rarely encounter such people. For the most part, we see individuals who act on their impulses. In fact, some offenders will admit to the molestation of scores of children. Able, Becker, Mittelman, Cunningham-Rathner, Rouleau, and Murphy (1987) reported that offenders in treatment who were sexually oriented to young males would admit to an average of 150 victims. Some of the individuals in this study claimed to have abused hundreds of boys (Able et al., 1987). Clearly, failing to document abuse in a single case can lead to the victimization of many other children.

Where once the public and many investigators thought of child molesters as strangers lurking in the park, it is now clear that most people who sexually abuse children are known to their victims. Most reports involve an adult or adolescent who abuses legitimate authority or an established relationship to access a child sexually (Faller, 1990). The suspect is often a family member, someone living in the home, or someone who has access to the child in a formal or informal supervisory role.

At the other end of the continuum are stranger abductions followed by sexual assaults, which are often high-profile cases for law enforcement. An estimated 3,200 to 4,600 stranger abductions occur each year in the United States. Most of these involve sexual assault, and between 43 and 147 each year end as homicides. Compared to the hundreds of thousands of child sexual abuse reports, these figures appear small, but the potential for even this form of the crime is not insignificant, with an estimated 114,600 annual attempts at such abductions (Finkelhor, Hotaling, & Sedlak, 1992). Even an attempt can have grave emotional consequences.

Ironically, despite the widespread nature of the problem of child sexual abuse and the strong criminal laws against this type of behavior, we still find some who question why it should receive priority attention from law enforcement and even child protection agencies. Many sexual assaults of children do not leave any lasting physical trauma, and the physical pain associated with the offense may be temporary. The trauma related to this form of abuse actually is greatest on the psychic level (Briere & Runtz, 1993).

Child sexual abuse often leaves lifelong scars. Even a single incident can linger in a survivor's mind for years, undermining his or her abilities to form and maintain relationships. The long-range effects of abuse of this nature have been debated over the years, but clearly adults who were molested as children are significantly more likely to experience cognitive distortions, adult sexual disturbance, anxiety, fear, depression, dissociative disorders, eating disorders, post-traumatic stress symptoms, and suicidal thoughts (Beitchman et al., 1992; Briere & Runtz, 1993). The pain is real and often profound.

Confronting this problem involves a diverse set of actors. In all 50 states, child protection agencies were established more than 25 years ago. Each is unique in its organization, mission, structure, and statutory authority. For some, the mission is limited to cases when direct family members are the alleged perpetrators. Others are charged by their state legislatures far more broadly to respond to allegations of sexual abuse regardless of the identities of the perpetrators, even if strangers. Although all of these agencies share federal mandates to avoid out-of-home placement where possible, some have even stronger state legislative direction to preserve families where possible.

❑ Child Protective Services

Most child protection agencies experienced enormous increases in demands in the 1980s without any significant increases in staff resources. In fact, child abuse reports were up 40% nationwide between 1985 and 1991, while 35 states reported level funding or significant reductions in resources (Child Welfare League of America, 1992). These agencies seek to address the needs of sexually abused children with increasingly limited reserves.

Making the problem worse is the reality that sexual abuse cases generally consume more resources than other forms of maltreatment. Child protection investigators can, for example, far more quickly assess the validity of a physical neglect case. The evidence in neglect cases often is clear on the first visit to the home. Even physical abuse cases are generally more straightforward. The investigator has visible trauma to work with and allied professionals such as physicians who can interpret the medical evidence. Sexual abuse cases generally represent less clear-cut situations. Often there is no clear medical finding of abuse. Rarely are there objective witnesses, because these assaults occur in private and are shrouded in secrecy. In the final analysis, investigating sexual abuse means interviewing all

> *Often there is no clear medical finding of abuse. Rarely are there objective witnesses.*

of the principals, sometimes more than once—a process that is, at best, time-consuming and requires the skillful application of the available knowledge.

❏ Law Enforcement

Law enforcement agencies also share responsibilities for responding to allegations of abuse. The sexual abuse of children is a crime in every jurisdiction in the nation. Although the statutory penalties are generally severe for this crime, it remains one of the most underinvestigated serious crimes on the books (Roberts, 1991). Historically, it is a crime that many law enforcement officers have deferred to child protection agencies, particularly if the offender is a family member.

The unique aspects of this form of criminal activity contribute to law enforcement attitudes. Child sexual abuse allegations are hard

to investigate and generally bring little prestige among fellow officers. The first dilemma that separates this crime from others is the
necessity to first prove that a crime has actually occurred. When
someone reports a burglary, police usually assume that the crime
occurred, unless evidence is produced to cast doubt on the report.
With child sexual abuse, the investigators often start with a less-than-
clear allegation. They must base their inquiry on the suspicions of
someone close to a child in whom the child has confided or on the
observations of such a person who reports behaviors indicative of
sexual victimization.

Next, even if the child discloses abuse, his or her language and
cognitive limitations (such as those of a 3-year-old) may require the
officer to speak and understand on a level at which the child may not
comprehend. In fact, most officers are as unfamiliar with the language of small children as they are with that of a recent immigrant
from a non-English-speaking country. If investigators overcome that
disability through training and experience, they are confronted with
the inherent problems of children as witnesses. Most officers who do
this work can report several cases in which their investigative efforts
seemed for naught when the child could not stand the rigors of a
confrontational criminal prosecution.

❑ Other Actors in the Investigation

Other actors in the protection of children include prosecutors who
rarely encountered sexual assault cases in criminal courts until the
mid-1980s. This type of case presented prosecutors with challenges
never encountered before. Prosecutors must overcome the same
language barriers experienced by the investigators in communicat-
ing with children and then confront unique courtroom dilemmas.
Protecting child witnesses from the excesses of the court process
became a goal for many prosecuting attorneys in the 1980s. A changing set of statutory laws mixed with an evolving body of case law
required legal professionals to stay current in a way rarely encountered in other types of cases.

By the same token, mental health professionals entered this period with little documented clinical experience and even less quantitative research. The 1980s saw not only an explosion of knowledge about the phenomenon of child sexual abuse but also an increasing role—for right or wrong—for mental health clinicians in the investigative process and any resulting litigation. These changes, coupled with the dramatic increase in reported cases, have thrust the various mental health disciplines into a central role in the design and operation of the broader child protective system.

In this same revolutionary period, the role of medical practitioners also underwent fundamental changes. They, too, saw the growth in reports and encountered a rapidly expanding understanding of sexually related trauma to the genitalia of children. In fact, the state of knowledge changed so rapidly in the 1980s that what was accepted as fact in 1980 was considered obsolete by 1985. By 1990, the prevailing professional understanding had again evolved dramatically. Physicians, like other professionals, were called on to keep up with an ever-changing body of knowledge.

Others were influenced by the changing environment. Everyone from foster parents to sophisticated residential treatment agencies faced a revolution of sorts. Where recognized sexual abuse victims in placement had been rare, they became commonplace by the early 1990s. Caregivers also had to adjust their traditional services to meet the specialized needs of sexual abuse victims and, increasingly, the needs of adolescent and preadolescent sexual offenders. For the first time, the potential for real and erroneous allegations of sexual assault by caregivers was recognized. The residential care industry was irrevocably altered.

As the system charged with child sexual abuse investigation and intervention evolved over the past 10 to 12 years, it has become clear that no single discipline or agency can meet the needs of abused children and their families. Child protection staff members first recognized that they needed the expertise of medical professionals and mental health clinicians, along with substitute care providers, to meet the range of needs of their sexually abused clients.

By pooling their resources and expertise, a powerful team could emerge.

Law enforcement officers and prosecutors recognized the need for the involvement of medical practitioners in their prosecutions. By the mid-1980s, however, child protection workers and law enforcement officers began to recognize that, by pooling their resources and expertise, a powerful new team could emerge—a team that served the common goals of all agencies and, most important, the interest of the child victims of abuse. It is to the design, development, operation, and maintenance of these investigative teams that this book is aimed.

2

Building Teams

Given the unique investigative complexities described in the previous chapter, it is little wonder that the disciplines involved in the
child sexual abuse intervention system have increasingly come to
realize that they can maximize their resources only by coordinating
their efforts. The concept of using teams in child abuse intervention
is not new: The first multidisciplinary, hospital-based teams were
established in 1958 in Pittsburgh, Los Angeles, and Denver (Krugman,
1988). In recent years, the lessons of the hospital-based teams have
been applied in investigative settings. Each investigative agency has
unique strengths and authority, but individually none "has all the
tools needed" (Colorado Department of Social Services [CDSS], 1991).
Together, the involved disciplines have far more power to determine
what did or did not happen than the individual entities have in
acting independently.

❑ History of Cooperation:
Child Protective Services and Law Enforcement

The concept of joint investigation is not new and, in some form or fashion, joint efforts between law enforcement and child protective services (CPS) appear common in this country. A recent study by the Police Foundation involving 606 sheriff's and police departments revealed that 94% conduct at least occasional joint investigations with child protection agencies (Sheppard, 1992). The authors have traveled to many communities in all parts of the country and have been struck by the diversity of arrangements that local agencies will call *joint investigation* or *teamwork*. They range from sharing written case information or holding periodic meetings around specific high-profile cases to those communities where all the actors function as a cohesive unit. In the latter cases, such a team is truly more powerful than the individual components.

In some high-profile cases, teamwork is more powerful than the individual components.

The same Police Foundation study supports the suggestion that the arrangements that exist for "joint investigation" in many jurisdictions fall short of fully functioning teams that meet the needs of all involved. Indeed, the study found that only 44% of law enforcement respondents from larger departments found joint investigations, as they exist in their communities, to be helpful. On the other hand, of the 51 officers responding to another survey of investigators in Tennessee (where team investigation is a priority), 84% indicated that CPS and law enforcement teams improved the accuracy of investigation. Only one officer in the Tennessee survey actually disagreed with a statement about improved accuracy (14% expressed no opinion) (Tennessee Network for Child Advocacy, 1990).

Relationships between law enforcement and child protective services have evolved on several levels during more than 25 years of shared responsibility. Today, in most jurisdictions there are neglect and even abuse cases that are, for all practical purposes, the sole responsibility of the child protection agency. These typically involve cases where only minor injuries have been reported or where the CPS intervention is based purely on the risk of future injury. Other forms of maltreatment such as educational neglect or emotional abuse also often fall within this category. Many states have no requirement for reporting this type of allegation to law enforcement (Martin & Besharov, 1991). Even if reports were required for these types of cases, there is reason to believe that many law enforcement agencies would not respond because of staff limitations and the poor prospects of criminal prosecution.

There are, however, a variety of situations in which CPS and law enforcement do come into contact. Generally, one of the first steps in any child protection investigation is to see the child. At times, parents or other caregivers deny CPS workers access to the child. When confronted with this resistance, CPS staff often rely on the more generally accepted authority of law enforcement to gain access to the child. Even if a court order is necessary, the officer will be in a much stronger position to enforce the order.

As protective services emerged in the 1960s and early 1970s, the CPS agency often relied on law enforcement to remove a child from the home when necessary. This practice developed despite authority for CPS to act to remove children without police involvement in 20 states (Besharov, 1990). Again, the more universally accepted authority of law enforcement officers was perceived to facilitate what is often a highly emotional and physically volatile situation. Some child protection professionals also suggested that another benefit of this arrangement would be that the client would associate the adversarial nature of the removal with law enforcement, thereby making it easier for the CPS worker to enter into a "helping relationship" with the client. Undoubtedly, this subtle distinction is lost on many clients, who readily recognize that the CPS worker is at least a major actor in the decision to remove the child.

Increasingly, in recent years another role for law enforcement involvement in CPS investigations has emerged. The child protection worker, even on the most straightforward neglect cases, must sometimes go into some of the most violent neighborhoods of our cities. By the same token, the workers are often, by definition, dealing with unstable and violent people. They go to these situations un-

armed and generally without any special training in personal defense. Making matters worse in most communities is the fact that
these workers do this without any direct means of telecommunica-
tions. In this day of cellular phones and hand-held radio communication, CPS workers in rural areas are going to remote homes miles
from the nearest telephone to confront potentially dangerous adults
without backup or any means to summon help if needed. The
problem is just as acute in metropolitan areas, where the growing
violence of the drug culture exposes the CPS worker to intensified
risk. In these situations, CPS officials must rely on law enforcement
officers to accompany the worker and keep the situation as stable as
possible.

Traditionally, when both CPS and law enforcement responded to
a report of maltreatment, they conducted their respective investigations on parallel tracks. Each went about its business without coordinating efforts or sharing information. In the 1970s, and even today
in many jurisdictions, this was the predominant way of investigating
serious physical abuse and many forms of sexual abuse. This meant
that each witness, including the child, had to be interviewed sepa-
rately by both agencies. Because their efforts were not coordinated,
the varying pace of the investigators could produce conflict, such as
when a premature CPS interview with the alleged perpetrator resulted in the destruction of physical evidence.

Another variation of the CPS–law enforcement relationship is in
cases where law enforcement has principal responsibility. In these
cases, CPS is relegated to providing any information it may have in
the agency records that might be helpful to the investigation. Such
cases vary dramatically by state. In several states, CPS is limited
primarily to cases where relatives are the alleged perpetrators, whereas
elsewhere CPS shares sexual abuse investigative responsibility with
law enforcement for all types of allegations, including strangers.
Other situations in which law enforcement acts alone generally
include child homicides without surviving minor siblings and allegations of past sexual abuse by an adult who was abused as a child
(and where the statute of limitations has not expired).

The final variation of CPS and law enforcement involvement is the
team. The investigative team is the most complicated of these variations and the one with the greatest payoff for the child victims and

involved agencies. The successful team draws on a mutual support network that reaches beyond the mandated investigative agencies and includes prosecutors, medical professionals, mental health clinicians, and others, as needed.

❏ Teams

Investigative training teaches us to attempt to answer five pertinent questions: Who? What? When? Where? Why? (See Box 2.1.) When examining the entity of the multidisciplinary team, it is helpful to answer these key questions.

Box 2.1: Essential Questions About Teams

Who composes the team?
What are teams? What do they do?
When is the team concept to be used?
Where do teams work?
Why are teams the best way to investigate child sexual abuse?

WHY INVESTIGATIVE TEAMS?

Increasingly, those who are involved in investigations of child maltreatment recognize the need to maximize skillful interviewing, eliminate duplication of efforts, promote proper and expedient collection of physical evidence, and reduce the secondary trauma associated with the investigative process. By working together, team members can be more efficient by sharing investigative tasks, more effective by assigning tasks to the members best prepared to accomplish them, and less injurious to the child by reducing the number of duplicate contacts and by building stronger cases for protection and prosecution (with a resulting increase in pleas and reduced need for child testimony). By working together, the team can accomplish the goals of all investigative agencies in a more efficient manner and with enhanced results.

WHAT ARE TEAMS?

Teams are entities composed of professionals from varying disciplines and organizations. They bring a diversity of skills, backgrounds and training to the investigation, and the result is stronger than the individuals acting alone. Teams share a common mission, and the members identify themselves as part of a collective effort to protect children.

WHO COMPOSES THE TEAM?

Generally, we are referring to teams of at least child protective services workers and law enforcement officers. Teams also include prosecutors, and often mental health clinicians and occasionally others such as medical professionals. The teams we refer to in this book are field investigative teams rather than consultative teams, which exist in some communities to advise frontline investigators after the fact.

WHAT DOES THE TEAM DO?

All team members will not actually work all aspects of the case, but all will be actively involved in the coordination of the total process as it draws from the resources available to member agencies. In effect, each agency and individual has unique strengths, and the team concept allows their full exploitation. Individual shortcomings are minimized by the depth of the team's talents and skills. The investigative responsibility rests with the team as much as it does with individual investigators or their agencies.

WHERE HAVE INVESTIGATIVE TEAMS WORKED?

Investigative teams have been effective in several jurisdictions. In some places, such as Tennessee, the team concept is mandated by state law, and local agencies are guided and coordinated at the state level. In other states, the law supports team investigation (for example, Colorado Section 19-3-308(4)(a) CRS, 1990), and state-level interagency task forces provide direction. Other teams have been established without any formal legislative involvement. These teams exist because of the personal leadership of an individual or group of individuals. Such teams develop their own procedures and protocols and may seek support from statewide organizations. Locally inspired efforts have produced one of the premier models of effective team work, the Child Advocacy Center concept developed in Huntsville, Alabama. The center-based model fosters interdisciplinary cooperation while providing a "child friendly environment" at the center. In the final analysis, team investigations have worked in major metropolitan areas and in remote rural communities and depend more on the will of those involved than on legislation or funding. That will is challenged further when the team moves from talking about making it work to the actual operation of a multidisciplinary investigative team.

❑ Uneasy Alliance

Establishing teams is easier said than done. Getting people to work together as a team in any professional environment is challenging. One must address the interpersonal dynamics and work-style variations, even when the team exists within a single organization or discipline. In multidisciplinary investigative teams, major differences exist in the organizational cultures of law enforcement and child protection agencies. Adding to the stress are the divergent philosophies and orientations of the allied professionals involved in the broader team network. Child protection agencies are generally built on a social work model and have professional and legal pressures to focus on maintaining families, where possible. By contrast, law enforcement has a clearer mandate to gather evidence of criminal activity and, with the prosecutor, aggressively seek a conviction. The successful investigative team must recognize these differences and potential sources of conflict and meet them head on.

For the team to work, each discipline must seek to understand the unique perspective of the other. It is these special experiences and perspectives that give the team concept its strength. We do not propose to blend the disciplines into a homogeneous mix in which law enforcement officers are indistinguishable from CPS workers or the mental health perspective is identical to that of the prosecutor. Rather, we want to create a final product that retains the unique perspectives of all involved. By understanding why others believe and act as they do, we are better able to accept, if not always agree, with the action of other team members (Pence & Wilson, 1988).

MISSION AND PHILOSOPHY

Most CPS agencies operate in a so-called social work tradition. They generally see themselves as part of a helping system that seeks to strengthen the ability of families to care for their own children. They sometimes are less comfortable with their roles as agents of social control. CPS agencies, in fact, do have a dual mission as embodied in state and federal law. On the one hand, they are responsible for protecting children from maltreatment at the hands of some statutorily defined set of persons. This daunting task entails investigation and the careful assessment of the risk of future abuse or neglect. On the other hand, the same agencies are charged with preserving the very family that abused the child (Faller, 1990).

Law enforcement's mission in these cases is more straightforward. It investigates crime by gathering facts and drawing logical conclusions to determine, in fact, whether a crime has been committed and by whom. When confronted with a case of child sexual abuse, most officers see criminal prosecution and incarceration as the desired outcome. They often find any interest on the part of CPS to preserve the family abhorrent. Law enforcement officers often feel the parents had their chance at raising the child and that they chose to use the child for their own or someone else's sexual gratification. Now they feel the parents do not deserve another opportunity to care for the child. If the child is placed in foster care, any discussion about reunification meets with the same level of outrage. Officers view punishment as a priority over social service delivery as a means of curtailing abuse (Trute, Adkins, & MacDonald, 1992).

These differences in mission and organizational philosophy can be a source of strife on the team. The caseworker particularly may be sensitive about these issues and indignant comments by officers. He or she may envy the clarity of mission of the law enforcement officer. The worker also has talked with the child and felt the same human outrage at the pain inflicted. He or she may well agree on a personal level that the parents deserve little consideration, but the worker may also have statutorily defined responsibilities to try to work with the family.

Differences in mission and organizational philosophy can be a source of strife on the team.

Furthermore, the caseworker is generally far more acutely aware of the problems with the alternative living situations to the child's home. For most children, removal from the home means placement with relatives or in foster care. To the child both these alternatives, with the accompanying changes in caretakers, school, sibling relationships, and friends, as well as the fear of the unknown, may be undesirable. In today's foster care system, there are too few foster homes, so those available in many jurisdictions tend to be overcrowded. Foster placement means that sibling groups often are split apart, and children who may have been severely traumatized by the abuse are retraumatized by being moved from one foster home to another because of their abuse-related behavior problems. Officers and other team members are less acutely aware of the adverse effects of foster care, may advocate for quicker reliance on placement, and resist the idea of reunification with the nonoffending parent, even if the offender is out of the home.

DIFFERENT DECISION-MAKING STYLES

Law enforcement officers are accustomed to rapid, autonomous decision making. Officers do not typically seek out the opinions of their superiors before acting in the field. Many CPS agencies, however, have developed a shared decision-making system. This translates into the need for the worker to consult by phone with a supervisor or perhaps the agency attorney before making selected key decisions such as removing a child. Police officers find this need to consult frustrating and inefficient. They may find their frustration soaring if the supervisor overrides the judgment of the officer and worker on the scene. CPS agencies, on the other hand, find this consultative style of decision making useful in avoiding overactions based on the emotions of the moment.

MULTIPLE LAW ENFORCEMENT JURISDICTIONS

An incongruence between the geographic jurisdictions of the local CPS agency and law enforcement agencies can create confusion. Where both share common boundaries, there is little room for confusion as to whom to contact, but a county divided into many separate police jurisdictions may well undermine the team concept. Unless adjustments are made, the team will be composed of an ever-changing cast of actors, some of whom will work so few cases that they will never develop the necessary expertise. Without coordination, the agencies involved may pass the buck or work at cross-purposes on cases that blend jurisdictional boundaries.

FAMILY CONTACT

A related issue that sometimes produces conflict on teams is the nature of family contact for a child victim who has been placed in foster care. Traditional child welfare thinking is that early and frequent visitation with the family from which the child is removed is in the child's best interest. Child welfare professionals have found that children isolated from the world they knew, both good and bad, tend to be more traumatized by the foster care experience than those who are able to have contact in a safe way with their parents and siblings. Isolation tends to lead to idealization of the parents and minimalization of the problems, and it contributes to a possible recantation of the allegation. In addition, the family or juvenile court may routinely order visitation, even if supervised. Law enforcement officers and prosecutors, on the other hand, may strongly oppose any family contact, fearing the family will use the opportunity to pressure the child to recant the allegations. In fact, given the opportunity, many families will do exactly what the officers fear, while isolating the child will have the adverse consequences feared by CPS.

DISPOSITION

Many new teams must confront real or anticipated differences in what the team members perceive as the desired case outcome. Law enforcement officers entering this work generally see long-term incarceration of the offender as the desired outcome. In fact, they may harbor a desire to deliver themselves what Pence calls "blue steel therapy." If treatment is to be provided to the offender, most officers will initially support its delivery only in prison. The idea of diversion, suspended sentences, probation, or parole-based treatment is often rejected. For many social workers, the desired outcome may be the elimination of abuse in the home and preservation of the family if feasible and safe. If this can be accomplished without criminal sanctions or through the use of community-sentencing alternatives, then new CPS team members may find themselves advocating for the least drastic alternative. Whether or not the actors play these stereotypical roles is less important at the outset of team formation than the process the team develops to resolve these conflicts.

In reality, the team experience tends to draw the divergent points of view closer together. The "hawks" on the team quickly realize that too few offenders actually spend any significant time behind bars and even fewer remain behind bars until they are no longer threats to children. With experience, these officers may conclude that the most important outcome is the prevention of future abuse. The "doves" on the team

> *The team experience tends to draw divergent points of view closer together.*

also learn that the offender-treatment process is enhanced through ties to the coercive power of the criminal justice system wherever possible. It also does not take teams too long to encounter an offender whose sexual orientation to children is so entrenched or his impulse control so low that all agree the only way protect the children is to incarcerate the individual for as long as possible.

MEASURES OF TEAM SUCCESS

On the front end, the team needs to agree on its mission and what constitutes success. The CPS worker might measure success as a thorough investigation, a sense that an accurate determination of what happened was made, and that the risk of further abuse has been controlled. The officer or prosecutor, however, might see his or her efforts as successful only if a criminal conviction is obtained. If all parties stick to these standards, then they will probably be frustrated. The team needs to recognize the importance of accurately determining that abuse did not occur, if that is the case, and take pride in sorting out valid cases from those that should not be substantiated. In intrafamilial cases, the criminal justice professionals must also see their role in protecting children in juvenile or family court as vital even if no criminal prosecution occurs. Mature teams tend to have CPS workers invested in gaining criminal convictions in those cases that the teams decide to pursue, while law enforcement officers are vitally interested in children's safety and well-being even when no charges are sought.

WORK-STYLE DIFFERENCES

Once teams work through the organizational and professional conflicts, they confront the interpersonal issues that can undermine the effectiveness of the team. One such issue is work-style differences. Some investigators are so-called Type A in orientation and anxious to get on with the investigation. These folks have little patience for much front-end planning or information processing. They tend to move rapidly from one interview to another without pausing to assimilate the data. The same orientation may spill over into the actual interview style. Some interviewers feel a need to get right to the issue with a child, leaving little time to develop rapport with the child or to assess the child's general developmental level.

Other investigators move at a slower pace, the so-called Type B individuals. These folks tend to want to plan things more and to take time between interviews to process what has been learned. These investigators are more comfortable with slower-paced interviews that allow the child time to acclimate. When Type A and Type B people are paired on a team, they must learn to accommodate each other's needs and styles or they risk frustration and confusion. They must also learn how to take advantage of the diversity, using the differing styles as a strength to be exploited by the team.

CULTURAL COMMUNICATION

People of both genders and of different racial or ethnic groups may communicate in ways that can lead to team conflict. These differences are well documented elsewhere. For example, women may ask questions of peers to initiate a discussion even when they are not seeking specific guidance. Men tend to assume that anyone asking a question wants direction about how to proceed (Tannen, 1990). Female team members may raise an issue with male team members (or vice versa) in a manner that results in a mutually unsatisfactory interchange. Even the way in which one gender communicates a request for action to the other can lead to conflict. For example, women tend to phrase such requests in a way that males are inclined to perceive as an order, one that they may be inclined to resist (Tannen, 1990). Sometimes, it is not necessarily the wording of the question, but the tone of voice that is interpreted as commanding and which rankles: "Jack, would you go in and get that offender file?" Similar problems exist in communications between members of different racial or ethnic groups. Where there are generational differences between team members, friction also has been noted and can become a serious problem.

REAL OR PERCEIVED INTERPERSONAL PROBLEMS

Teams are composed of different disciplines and often different genders (see Box 2.2). The differing organizational cultures of these agencies might also lead to misunderstanding, particularly in combination with gender or racial differences. For example, it might be standard practice at the sheriff's department to gather at a local bar for drinks after the shift to "decompress." A male deputy might innocently invite the new female CPS team member to the bar to join in the ritual. Unfamiliar with the culture of the sheriff's office, the female caseworker might believe the invitation is sexually oriented, leading to a strained working relationship as she attempts to avoid what she perceives as an awkward personal situation.

Box 2.2:
Types of Interpersonal Problems Encountered

Honest misunderstandings
Sexual harassment
Sexual involvements
Racism
Divergent ages
Sexism

On the other hand, the interactions between male and female team members can cross the line into consensual sexual involvements that may serve to affect adversely the objective balance of the team. Unfortunately, some interactions between members of the opposite sex can become sexual harassment. One example reported to the authors was of a male officer who whispered sexually suggestive comments in the ear of the female social worker while she was using an anatomically detailed doll in a child interview. The behavior was widely discussed, with the result that no female CPS worker in the county wanted to work with the officer.

Similar problems, real and perceived, can arise among members of different racial or ethnic groups. The use of racial stereotypes or slang can quickly undermine a relationship, just as the misinterpretation of an innocent statement by a new team member can produce strained relationships on the team.

Divergent ages represented on the team also can cause some conflict. Older personnel may have little appreciation for the "fledglings" on the team. They may devalue, consciously or unconsciously, the contributions of these younger members and, if possible, assign them to the least significant tasks. Although we recognize the need for new people to become oriented and educated and find their "sea legs," they will never develop professionally or become respected team members until they are "mentored" appropriately.

Conversely, some younger individuals come to the team full of enthusiasm and ideas but with little grounding. They may be reluctant to accept the experience and wisdom of those who have more experience. The slower pace with which some of their older counterparts move is frustrating. The newer members may not yet have developed an appreciation for the beneficial ebbs and flows of a successful investigation.

We have also noted on teams a situation that Pence has labeled the "my girl syndrome." When speaking to male team members, particularly law enforcement officers, Pence noted that some praised the teams highly and viewed them as unqualified successes. When pressed to explain what contributed to the success, many of these men praised their working relationships with female social counselors or mental health therapists. They commonly expressed variations on this theme: "My girl is great. She will do anything I want her to do. If I need something done, all I have to do is tell her and it gets taken care of." This type of attitude does not speak well for the balance of power on the team. The female co-workers of these men did not have the same rosy view of the team functioning. Almost universally, they felt like drones or administrative assistants to the males. They are not happy campers. A few "traditionalist" women are comfortable with this style of relationship, but this is not the norm and should not be encouraged or tolerated by supervisors. This dynamic reduces the likelihood of full participation by valuable members and sets the stage for successors to start out trapped in an unfulfilling role.

❑ Addressing the Problems

Recognizing the possible sources of conflict can help the team avoid problems in functioning. Recognition alone is not enough, however. Professionals establishing teams can take assertive action to improve team operation at both the system and personal levels. If the conflict is minimized and diversity properly channeled, the investigative goals of all involved can be achieved and the secondary traumatization of the victim in the investigative process can be minimized.

SYSTEM RECOMMENDATIONS

Implementation of the following recommendations will help to ensure the team's smooth and effective functioning:

- Establish formal teams
- Understand and use team dynamics
- Establish investigative protocol
- Provide adequate personnel
- Provide joint training
- Engage in team building

Establishing Formal Teams

Much of the conflict is exacerbated when individuals rarely work together. Trust and predictability that comes from working together over time allows individuals to look beyond issues of acute disagreement. Teams can formalize themselves through a combination of predictable membership (and a resulting sense of belonging to the team) and development of predictable behaviors such as meeting times, places, structure, and formal agreements on roles or duties. Teams can be established on a community basis (e.g., DuPage County, Illinois) or across an entire state by statutory direction (e.g., Tennessee).

Understanding and Using Team Dynamics

The development of teams goes through stages sometimes referred to as "forming, storming, norming, and performing." In the first stage, *forming*, team members are learning skills and roles, testing one anothers' commitment, and defining the tasks. In the next stage, *storming*, a new team often competes for control: It may set unrealistic goals, focus on tasks over outcomes, and make little real progress. During the *norming* stage, the team members begin to give and accept feedback and share ideas while setting realistic operational norms and actually making progress. Finally, the team moves into the *performing* stage, in which it diagnoses and overcomes operational problems while using feedback to make changes and continuously improve performance.

Looking at it another way, the team is making the transition from a working group to a fully effective team. The working group usually has a strong focused leader and each individual is accountable independently and maintains his or her individual work products. With teams, leadership is shared, accountability is both individual and mutual, and work products are collective (Katzenbach & Smith, 1993). The process of this transition has been visualized in phases: the *work group,* the *pseudo team,* the *potential team,* and the real team (Katzenbach & Smith, 1993). The team needs to anticipate this process and allow enough time to work through normal developmental stages.

Struggles for leadership can be particularly destructive, and the team needs to decide who will convene the team and chair its meetings. Using the relatively neutral mental health member might be a good compromise. If the team is perceived by most agencies as under the control of one person or discipline, such as the prosecutor, then others' levels of commitment may be diminished. The team must belong to all.

Once operational, the team can anticipate numerous challenges. One of the most common is the introduction of a new member after a veteran departs. It is natural for the new person to question the way things are done, and it is equally normal for the rest of the team to resent the challenge to the status quo. The team must prepare for any changes in personnel and help the new member to acclimate to team operations.

Another challenge is the way in which the team handles adverse publicity. If news media can generate or orchestrate divisions between the disciplines, then the old "divide and conquer" effect may work. Effective teams need to recognize that all publicity will not be good and prepare for the inevitable in a positive fashion. It is best not to believe that one team member has made a particular comment to the news media until it is directly confirmed in person. Other team challenges include maintaining energy over time, the involvement of new supervisory or management personnel, and changes in agency priorities. Each requires the team to develop a careful strategy that will overcome the emerging barrier to success.

Establishing Multijurisdictional Teams Where Needed

In those communities with many small police jurisdictions, follow the experience of multijurisdictional drug task forces and allow experienced officers to work across jurisdictional boundaries. Nationally, there are more than 1,000 such drug task forces (Levine & Martin, 1992), and the same level of cooperation needs to be applied to sexual abuse investigation. Where multijurisdictional drug, drunk driving, or gambling task forces or teams exist, the process needs to be studied and duplicated, if at all possible. What kinds of agreements were necessary? What level of hierarchy was necessary to get the job done? Would getting the public involved help the process? Can the need be established as a result of "botched" or inefficient investigations? Will the prosecutor's office be a strong supporter and participant? What are the logistical impediments to be tackled and overcome? Are there any funding sources that could help sell the concept?

Establishing Investigative Protocols

Investigative protocols clearly lay out standard operating procedures and roles for the various team members. As described in Chapter 4, the protocol need only serve as a basis of interaction; the team should be free to modify it to unique case situations.

Tennessee's state protocol, for instance, calls for the team to interview the alleged victim before the child's parents. Specific circumstances, however, may dictate a deviation from normal practice: For example, in an out-of-home perpetrator case, the team might first interview the parents about the child's contacts with the suspect.

Providing Adequate Personnel for All Team Agencies

When one agency commits significantly more staff resources to the team than the other—typically, either CPS or law enforcement—it sets itself up to do a disproportionate share of the work. Beyond the inequity of this, it may well mean that one agency ends up triaging cases, with those considered serious receiving follow-up interviews and contacts from the whole team or, even worse, the other agency alone. In such cases, the efficiencies of the team are lost, and the victim and others must endure several interviews. Additional problems can arise such as CPS staff members being unable to wait for law enforcement to interview the alleged perpetrator and thus proceeding and inadvertently confounding the delayed criminal investigation. In fact, shortages of law enforcement personnel were cited as a barrier to effective joint investigation by more than 57% of CPS and law enforcement agencies surveyed by the Police Foundation. Similar concerns were expressed about CPS in more than 40% of the respondents to the same survey (Sheppard, 1992).

Joint Training

Joint training is one of the keys to effective multidisciplinary teams (Pence & Wilson, 1988). Experience tells us that the joint training is essential in implementing interagency agreements and should be delivered before team operations begin (Martin & Besharov, 1991). This type of training helps the team member understand the nature of the member agencies' respective missions and philosophies. Many of the potential system conflicts can be brought into the open and discussed in the relatively objective environment of the training. In one state, law enforcement routinely expressed frustration that CPS workers inadvertently spoiled crime scenes. After joint training, CPS workers became aggressive in encouraging proper collection of physical evidence. Conversely, joint training helped law enforcement officers understand the legal mandates for "reasonable efforts to prevent removal" of even sexually abused children from their homes.

Team Building

At any stage in the team's development, it can benefit from activities designed to build team cohesion. This can take the form of simple recreational activities or shared professional experiences. It also can include exercises that help the team to better understand individual communication styles and personality traits. One such process that investigative teams in several states have used is the Myers-Briggs Type Indicator (Myers, 1987).

❑ Individual Recommendations

The following recommendations also may help team members work more effectively with one another:

- Become educated about other disciplines
- Develop personal relationships
- Share professional literature
- Keep communications open
- Confront problems openly
- Keep supervisors involved

SELF-EDUCATION

Each member needs to learn more about the culture of the other team agencies, including how they operate and what they value. If members work with the other gender or members of another race or ethnic group, then they should seek out ways to enhance cross-gender or cross-cultural communication. In some cases this will not be a problem, but in others it can seriously undermine the team. The individual should adjust his or her conduct to minimize behavior that is offensive to other team members.

DEVELOPING PERSONAL RELATIONSHIPS

Each member should get to know other members on a personal level, including about their families and how they spend their personal time. At the same time, members should demonstrate that they see others as professional colleagues.

SHARING PROFESSIONAL LITERATURE

Sharing professional literature such as books, articles, legal analyses, and even agency operations manuals with those in other disciplines educates other team members while sending the message that they are viewed as colleagues.

KEEPING COMMUNICATION OPEN

Even if formal protocols do not require it, the team should be kept current on case events such as court dates and decisions (criminal as well as juvenile), decisions about family visitation or reunification, and investigative contacts.

CONFRONTING PROBLEMS OPENLY

Inevitable conflicts should be addressed in a nonthreatening yet straightforward manner. The issue should be on the table for the entire team to discuss. Some issues can be resolved, whereas the team may agree to disagree on others. Even a heated discussion in a team meeting is better than a heated discussion at 10 p.m. in the emotionally laden atmosphere of an investigation. Disagreements are to be expected even in the most successful teams.

KEEPING SUPERVISORS INFORMED
AND INVOLVED

The agency supervisors should feel free to attend team meetings and schedule periodic meetings to evaluate team operations. Supervisors need to remain responsible for ensuring that their agency representative(s) support the team concept and mission. When anticipated, the varying missions, philosophies, and procedures of the member agencies or the occasional misunderstandings of persons of divergent backgrounds and styles need not present an insurmountable barrier to team operation. In fact, diversity is what makes the team concept so powerful. Communication at both the system and personal levels is the key to making interagency teams work. When teams fail because of these problems, we are generally no worse off than before we tried the team concept. When the team concept works, it works for the involved agencies, for the individual professionals working on the team, and, most important, for the young victims of child sexual abuse.

3

Roles and Responsibilities

The team concept draws its strength not just from the additional investigative personnel it brings to the task but also, and more important, from the richness that comes from the combined knowledge and skills of multiple disciplines and the diversity of authority invested in the member agencies. When we establish teams and crosstrain their members, we are not seeking to make police officers of the social workers or social workers of the cops. Indeed, for the team concept to work properly, it is vital that team members maintain their individuality and function within broad role constraints.

Team members must maintain individuality and function within broad role constraints.

All team members do not participate in each aspect of the investigation, but together they coordinate the total process, drawing from the resources available. First, teams quickly find obvious areas of overlap where the team roles become interchangeable (e.g., interviewing children). With these tasks, the team has flexibility to assign responsibility based on personal and professional strengths and experience. Second, in other areas (e.g., interviewing suspects) one agency will logically take the lead by virtue of its organizational authority and specialized training and experience. A third category is also present in which the unique legal authority vested in a specific agency or subset of agencies (crime scene searches by law enforcement) requires that it or they be the only ones involved in certain activities. The roles of each member must be understood by the other team members at the beginning. Failure to do so invites conflict over who is responsible for which aspect of the investigation and the resulting loss of efficiency and effectiveness.

The roles of the team members are varied and can be broken down by discipline. Where the same activity appears without comment in more than one discipline, assume that the team can assign that duty based solely on individual experience and skill. Of course, when dividing duties among team members, it is critical to remember that the team member performing that task is doing so not only on behalf of his or her individual agency but also on behalf of the team. It is important that the member know and gather the information needed by the other disciplines to avoid the need for repeated contacts.

Investigative teams take many forms and involve different agencies, depending on the jurisdiction and the specifics of the case. As a general rule, the primary field investigators of the teams discussed in this book are composed of child protection staff and law enforcement officers. Depending on the case, the team also may include state or federal law enforcement agencies. Functioning behind the scenes are the prosecutor and the attorney who represents the CPS agency in juvenile or family court in any dependency action. Many teams also include a mental health professional who may only provide guidance or assist in team coordination or actually see the child in a forensic or extended assessment role. These disciplines represent the principal team members. Other professionals may assist in the investigation temporarily and become members of an extended team, including medical professionals performing sexual abuse examinations, other mental health professionals working with the child, and even the substitute care provider for a child in foster or residential care.

Box 3.1: The Role of Child Protective Services

The child protective services agency and worker:
1. accepts reports of abuse
2. interviews alleged child victims
3. interviews siblings or other possible child witnesses
4. interviews nonoffending parent(s)
5. interviews other adult witnesses and collateral contacts
6. interviews the alleged offender if the team determines this to be appropriate (such an interview is typically performed by law enforcement personnel)
7. arranges medical examination and psychological examinations of child and parents, if needed
8. performs risk assessment (an analytical process to assess the likelihood of future abuse)
9. develops a safety plan to protect the child in his or her home or the home of a relative or family friend
10. petitions the juvenile or family court (through the attorney representing the agency) for custody to place the child in foster care
11. secures a foster home or other appropriate placement
12. develops a case plan to meet the child's needs and reduce the risk of future abuse
13. arranges community services to support the plan such as counseling or financial support for the mother if the offender has moved out of the home
14. evaluates the service delivery process and the progress or lack of progress by the involved family member
15. testifies in court proceedings (juvenile, family, or criminal court as well as grand juries if appropriate) and makes recommendations to the court about the long-term plan for permanence for the child

---

In many communities, the CPS worker comes to the team with more experience and training in interviewing children than is typical of law enforcement officers, who come to the team from patrol work or other investigative duties (see Box 3.1). With the rapid growth in reports in recent years and the corresponding increase in knowledge and training, the expertise of investigative interviewing among CPS workers has improved (Faller, 1990). For these reasons, child protection workers often take the lead in interviewing alleged victims and other child witnesses. It should be noted that the individual expertise of specific team members varies, and the law enforcement member of the team may actually have far more training and experience in talking with children. In that case, the team would have the officer take the lead in the interview. As we will see later, joint interviews with both law enforcement and CPS present can be very effective if handled right.

The assessment of risk is one area in which child protection generally takes the lead, with input from other team members. Such risk assessment systems as Action for Child Protection's Child at Risk Field are designed to attempt to structure the decision-making process in a way that minimizes the likelihood of repeated abuse or overreaction by an inexperienced worker. Some systems—such as those in Florida, Tennessee, and Illinois—also serve to guide the service delivery process throughout the life of the case. There is nothing magical about these efforts. They are simply examining the various factors that place the child at risk, first in isolation (i.e., infants are inherently at greater risk than teenagers, given that all other factors are equal) and then in combination (i.e., an infant in the hands of a psychotic father with a history of sexual assault who lives on a remote farm). (See Box 3.2.)

Box 3.2: Risk Factors in Sexual Abuse

The following risk factors are particularly relevant in sexual abuse cases:

1. a history of sexually abusive behavior that demonstrates sexual interest and the capacity to act on that interest
2. the presence of someone with an abusive capacity in the home or the degree of their access to the child
3. the degree of isolation present in the child, factors that influence impulse control, and the influence of inhibitions such as substance abuse, mental illness, or significant mental retardation
4. the level of belief primary caretakers have that the risk of abuse is real and that the child needs protection from a specific person whom they have previously trusted
5. the ability of a nonoffending parent to protect the child

Good risk assessments also consider family strengths that may balance some of the risks. The final risk judgments take all these factors into account and drive the safety plan decisions (e.g., what must change for the child to remain in the home or be safe at a relative's home?) or the judgment to legally remove the child from the home. Risks and strengths also guide the service delivery that targets specific risk-reduction services such as addressing substance abuse or building on strengths such as a mother's ability to accept responsibility for protecting the child. Ultimately, risks and strengths drive decisions about reunification or termination of parental rights.

The worker's interview with nonoffending parents is designed to gather facts about the alleged abuse and to provide information for the risk assessment process. The child protective services worker also may wish to seek out other relatives or collateral contacts to gather data for this process. Even elements of the confrontation interview with the alleged offender will be useful to the risk analysis.

The CPS staff also will play a dominant role in establishing a safety plan, if necessary. This is the plan of protection for the child during the investigative process. For example, CPS may quickly assess the safety of a temporary relative placement after an initial disclosure, or it may determine the practicality of an alleged perpetrating father voluntarily moving out of the home until the investigation is complete.

❏ Understanding the Limits of the Role of Child Protection

Some team tasks may exceed the statutory authority of the child protection agency and turn the CPS staff into agents of law enforcement. For example, when the team is present in the home and the officer has a search warrant or a consent to search, then CPS workers should not participate in the search because it goes beyond their statutory authority and as such may expose them to personal legal liability.

In a similar vein the officer must not attempt to avoid search limitations by having CPS workers ask parents to let the workers take evidence with them only to turn it over to law enforcement once out the door.

Another area that presents potential problems is the interview with the alleged perpetrator. Although certainly nothing is wrong if the team decides to have the CPS worker conduct the interview with the alleged offender, it does not alter the need to inform the suspect of his or her legal rights per Miranda, if the interview is conducted in a custodial setting or one in which a reasonable person would believe that he or she is not free to leave. If the suspect is otherwise entitled to Miranda, then the courts have viewed the CPS worker as an agent of law enforcement and have excluded confessions secured by CPS [*People v. Kerner*, Ill. Apprd., 528 NE 2nd 1223 (1989); *Cates v. State* No. 031-088 (Texas, 1989); and *Tenn. v. Loveday*, Ct of Criminal Appeals, East (1990)]. The team must set limits on the roles of team members consistent with statutory authority, case law, and common sense.

❏ The Role of Law Enforcement

The law enforcement officer generally:

1. responds to calls in an appropriate manner (that is, one commensurate with the urgency of the call), stabilizes the crime scene, and takes initial statements as appropriate;
2. performs criminal history record checks on alleged offenders;
3. collects and preserves physical evidence (e.g., trace evidence or instruments used in the assault);
4. interviews child victims or witnesses consistent with the team's decision;
5. conducts photo lineups or live lineups to confirm the identification of perpetrators, if necessary;
6. interviews adult witnesses in cooperation with CPS;
7. facilitates the use of technological investigative tools such as monitored telephone conversations;
8. interviews alleged perpetrators;
9. takes suspects into custody, when and if appropriate;
10. presents criminal cases in lawsuits:
    a. to obtain warrants;
    b. to grand juries, if used in jurisdiction;

      c. at preliminary hearing, if appropriate;

      d. in criminal court;

11. testifies in juvenile or family court, if necessary, to ensure the child's protection; and

12. takes child into protective custody if the CPS worker assesses that the risks require the child's removal.

Law enforcement brings to the team expertise in collecting and preserving evidence, examining crime scenes, taking statements, and securing confessions. The law enforcement officer also is able to make arrests and is best able to present the criminal case in the appropriate forums because of his or her training and familiarity with criminal law and procedures (Pence & Wilson, 1992). The law enforcement agency also has greater access (directly or through the state law enforcement agency) to technological equipment and the skilled personnel who use it. This includes a range of devices, from sophisticated pinhole surveillance cameras, to simpler telephone monitoring and recording equipment, to the equipment needed to reduce the background noise that makes an audiotape of a child interview difficult to hear.

In defining team roles, the discussion within the team should consider all investigative agency personnel that the child and family will encounter. Although not formally part of the investigative team, patrol officers often become involved in these cases through their response to domestic calls. In some jurisdictions, they are routinely dispatched as first responders. In fact, 78% of the law enforcement agencies responding to a national survey by the Police Foundation reported that they sent a patrol unit to the scene to conduct an initial investigation when a call came in to the dispatcher. Only 14% of the respondents sent a specialized unit as a first responder, even though 92% reported having one or more "specialists" in either a criminal investigation unit or in the juvenile services division (Martin & Besharov, 1991). If this practice occurs within a community attempting to establish teams, it is important that the patrol officers have clearly defined roles and related training. In Montgomery County,

> *The team defines roles for all investigative agency personnel.*

Maryland; San Francisco; and Washtenaw County, Michigan, for example, patrol officers contact abuse specialists as soon as it is apparent that they are dealing with probable allegations of abuse. "This arrangement has produced fewer victim interviews and stronger cases. Also, the frequency of contacts among a few persons in each agency has fostered closer cooperation and the development of trusting relationships between police and child protective agency personnel" (Martin & Besharov, 1991).

With these experiences in mind, the role of patrol officers needs to be clearly defined. The dispatcher should have a protocol that defines when a patrol unit should be sent to the scene before the team. This could include incidents in which the speed of arrival is vital to child protection (i.e., the child is being abused at the moment the call comes in). Patrol officers need to have clear guidance on when to call the team and who at the law enforcement agency will contact child protective services. The uniformed officer also should be prepared to protect the crime scene, stabilize the situation by calming the family, assess any emergency medical needs for the child or others, and assess any risk of violence. The officer also should identify any possible witnesses on their arrival. But as a general rule, initiating a preliminary investigation should be avoided until the team is on the scene.

The officer on the team is then in a position to coordinate with CPS as to who takes the lead in talking with the child(ren), interviewing witnesses, and conducting a specialized search when there is consent to search or a search warrant. This team member often selects the time and place for the confrontation with the offender and conducts the actual interview.

❑ The Role of the Prosecutor

The prosecutor will serve primarily in an advisory role helping guide the field investigators until the case is ready for disposition. The prosecutor will:

1. actively participate in developing the case's overall investigative strategy;
2. assess the evidence collected to determine its potential utility in court;

3. assist in drafting search warrants;
4. participate in suspect interview when appropriate;
5. give guidance on legal issues, such as statute of limitations problems and jurisdictional issues;
6. determine appropriate charges and the best means of charging (arrest vs. grand jury);
7. negotiate bail or plea agreements and restrictions;
8. prepare witnesses for court or oversee a court school program for children; and
9. present the state's case at trial.

In most jurisdictions, prosecutors function behind the scenes of investigations. Their familiarity with the law and potential defense tactics puts them in an excellent position to help develop investigative strategies. In some communities the prosecutor is much more involved in the investigative phase of the case. However, in most communities, the prosecutor really steps into the forefront when the case moves into the prosecutory phase where he or she assumes the central role in any plea negotiations, in ensuring that the child is prepared for court, and in presenting the state's case at trial, while at the same time seeking ways to reduce the trauma of this process to the child.

❏ The Role of the Child Welfare Agency Counsel

The legal representation of child protective service agencies varies dramatically around the country. Many agencies employ their own counsels, while others use county attorneys, the states' attorneys general offices, or, in some cases, attorneys who work out of prosecutors' offices. No matter how his or her role is configured, this professional plays a vital role in the team's effort to protect children.

This attorney's responsibilities include the following:

1. reviewing evidence to determine if sufficient reason exists to remove the child from the home, if that is what the CPS worker (and sometimes supervisor) feels is necessary;

2. preparing or supervising the preparation of petitions to the court for removal of a child, when necessary;
3. preparing petitions for no contact orders where appropriate;
4. presenting the state's case in juvenile or family court;
5. giving general legal advice about civil cases;
6. negotiating visitation arrangements with parents' attorneys, if necessary; and
7. preparing injunctions to prevent continued access to children by abusers, if needed.

The criminal justice process often moves slowly, and even after arrest, an offender might well be out on bail and representing a risk to the child. The dependency attorney can access the power of the juvenile or family court (depending on the state) to protect the child, and this attorney is critical in staving off efforts to force a premature reunification with the offender. This same individual may, in some cases, also be the attorney to present the team's case to an administrative tribunal as it considers a child care license of a person alleged to have committed sexual abuse within a licensed child care facility such as a day care center. In addition, this attorney will represent the team at the due process hearings, which have been established in some states for persons listed on the central child abuse registry, or in civil court when the CPS agency seeks an injunction against an individual to protect children. Ultimately, the attorney representing the CPS agency must coordinate closely with the criminal prosecutor to avoid conflicts in court orders or the use of the civil matter as a means of getting premature discovery of evidence in a criminal case.

❏ The Role of the Mental Health Representative

Mental health professionals can play many important roles on investigative teams. On the conservative level, they are trained to help bridge conflicts among the team members and focus on team building and maintenance activities. They also generally come to teams with the most advanced formal clinical training on child development and human behavior. With this background they are in a good position to help guide the actual interview strategies based on the child's developmental level.

The role of the mental health clinician in the investigative process includes:

1. providing guidance or suggestions on interviewing strategies for children that are specific to their developmental level, gender, and emotional state;
2. assisting in the interpretation of psychological information received by the team (e.g., explaining the implications of various *Diagnostic and Statistical Manual* (3rd ed., rev.) (*DSM-III-R*) diagnoses to the team as it evaluates the credibility of witnesses;
3. making treatment recommendations for children;
4. advising prosecutors on the appropriateness of community-based sentencing options for offenders;
5. conducting "evidentiary" or forensic interviews (Stephenson, 1992);
6. conducting extended assessments of the children; and
7. coordinating the team in general.

In some communities, mental health specialists take far more active roles. Whether they work for prosecutors or law enforcement (such as in Everett, Washington), a hospital-based center (as in San Diego, California), a Child Advocacy Center (Huntsville, Alabama), or for another community-based agency (Nashville, Tennessee), a specially trained mental health interviewer may be in the best position to build a relationship and secure an accurate account of what, if anything, has happened in the life of a child who seems reluctant to talk to investigators. Some specialists use a single evidentiary interview (San Diego), while others use a series of less-directive play interviews (Nashville and Huntsville). If the team wishes to include this component, it is important that the mental health interviewer clearly understands the nature of investigative questioning (a minimal use of leading questions) and the type of information needed by all involved agencies. It is important, too, that all understand the rules of confidentiality. Some well-respected mental health professionals working in the field of child sexual abuse are uncomfortable with this role, and conflict can be avoided by clear expectations on the front end.

❑ The Role of Medical Professionals

Medical professionals sometimes function as members of extended teams. This has distinct advantages: It provides a team with consistent information from a physician or specially trained nurse who understands the medical issues and can help the team understand the medical findings. As with other team members, frequent contact builds trust. The drawback to this arrangement, however, should not be dismissed lightly. The opinion of a medical clinician who is closely associated with the investigative team will be portrayed at trial by defense attorneys as biased in favor of the prosecution. Some teams prefer to develop a working relationship with a medical facility that has the needed equipment and trained staff but which remains independent of the team and its decision-making process.

The roles of medical professionals include:

1. interpreting medical findings to the team;
2. performing forensic medical examinations;
3. recording the verbal statements made by the children during the examination (which are admissible in some courts); and
4. preserving any physical evidence secured during the examination (e.g., semen) or any photographs taken of injuries.

❑ Others

The core team is composed of child protective services, law enforcement, the criminal prosecutor, and the CPS agency attorney. The inclusion of a mental health specialist makes the team more balanced, often adding expertise in a critical area. The medical evaluation is critical, but it does not have to be a formal part of the team.

The team also may wish to include other key actors as an extended team from which the core investigative team can gain valuable information. For example, the foster parents with whom the child is placed can be encouraged to document any spontaneous statements about the abuse made by the child. Professionals such as teachers, residential child care providers, or therapists are part of a service delivery team for the child after he or she enters care; if approached properly by the investigators, these adults can be excellent sources for understanding the evolving disclosure from the child.

Teams can and do work in a variety of configurations. Although desirable, it is not necessary to have a large center-based team with all the disciplines mentioned in this chapter actively involved. A single CPS worker working with a single law enforcement officer can make up a team. Teams have even worked when the only interested agencies were the prosecutor's office and the CPS agency. The key to team success is not just which individuals are on the team, but how well their respective roles are defined.

> *The key to team success is how well respective roles are defined.*

Without clear delineation of roles, someone will undoubtedly leave something undone that others expected, or he or she will engage in an activity that the others believe is beyond the individual's scope or abilities. The importance of mutual *under*standing of roles cannot be *over*stated, and the necessity of learning how to facilitate cooperation cannot be underestimated.

4

Investigative Protocols

One factor that contributes to successful teams is their predictability for those involved in the investigative process. Conflict is avoided if the participants do not have to negotiate every point for each referral. If team members know not only what is expected of them but also what to expect of their colleagues and what actions they can antici-pate, then they are better able to focus their energies on the task at hand.

The goal of the investigation is to determine if a child has been abused or is at imminent risk of being abused and, if so, by whom and what can be done to protect the child (or others) from more abuse. The means to this end may include criminal prosecution or juvenile court action, as well as the delivery of services to the child or a protective family. Throughout this process the team must bal-ance the evidence-gathering process with protecting the child's best interests (Goldstein, 1987). These goals can best be accomplished when the team is functioning within the parameters of a written investigative protocol—a protocol that provides predictability and direction to the investigation.

Protocols take many forms, and clearly no single investigative agreement or design will work equally well throughout the nation. Factors such as population density, legal authority of child protection, the number of law enforcement jurisdictions, the presence of federal reservations, and the degree of investigatory specialization will influence the nature of the agreement. The model that will work in San Francisco will not work in the hills of Tennessee or on a tribal reservation in Montana. Unique features of the investigative agency's organization and state law will likewise influence the working relationship and the types of cases to which it will be applied. The actual protocol in some ways is secondary to the process used to develop it (Colorado Department of Social Services [CDSS], 1991) and the mutual understanding it represents. When the Tennessee General Assembly passed legislation that mandated team investigation, officials from law enforcement, prosecutors' offices, child protection agencies, and mental health agencies sat down for the first time and found that they had far more in common than any had expected. After working on protocols together, the members and their agencies had formed strong relationships that have endured for more than nine years.

Protocols take two broad forms. First are those examples that use the protocol to articulate the interagency agreement. In the absence of a statutory mandate for team investigation, written interagency protocols are considered important to an improved response to child abuse (Martin & Besharov, 1991). Such protocols spell out the purpose of the agreement, the cases in which the protocol will be used, the nature of cross-reporting, and issues of team coordination such as the frequency of team meetings. Some establish time frames for initiating investigations or team staffings. The DuPage County, Illinois, agreement even stipulates that the investigative team comprise one male and one female investigator. Protocols should address how the team will function in the event one member agency is unduly delayed in

> *Protocols articulate interagency agreement and detail the investigative process.*

responding. This is an acute problem if the team cannot act until both CPS and law enforcement are available and yet one of these agencies cannot respond for several days. Such a delay would obviously endanger a child if the perpetrator had continued access. The protocol needs to clarify under what circumstances one agency can act without the other(s).

Interagency protocols should address procedural issues such as under what circumstances interviews will be video- or audiotaped and by whom. If this is done, then all members must agree on how the tapes will be maintained, by whom, and under what circumstances they will be shared with others. The agreement also can cover such items as the use of anatomically detailed dolls or other interviewing tools. A national multidisciplinary consensus-building meeting on this topic also suggested that the agreement needs to include criteria for child removal, criteria for arrest, and provisions for joint training (Besharov, 1990).

The other form of protocol actually details the investigative process that outlines the investigative steps to be undertaken and the order in which the team will typically approach them. As a statewide interagency task force in Colorado characterized it, the protocol "must balance the need for structure and direction with the need for flexibility and alternatives" (CDSS, 1991). Still, protocols can give the team a framework within which to work by outlining such issues as report taking, background checks, the order of interviews, evidentiary issues, and team decision-making processes.

In Colorado, the protocol gives only broad guidelines, leaving the details to be worked out locally. This style of protocol raises issues for the team such as the need to decide when to initiate the investigation, where to conduct initial interviews, who will take the lead in the interview for each person, and whether the interviews will be taped. To some degree, the Colorado guidelines lay out roles, including that of law enforcement in preserving evidence and that of CPS in risk assessment. The guidelines also stipulate the sharing of reports among the team, and they provide broad direction in issues of arrest and child removal.

In San Francisco, the protocols are broken into separate documents for in-home and out-of-home sexual abuse. Within these parameters, the protocol addresses the actual interview process, including where the interview should take place, the nature of the (age-appropriate) language used, and recantations by the child. In this community, the protocol directs the interviews to be audiotaped. The San Francisco protocol also directs the police member of the team, even at the earliest stage of the case, to urge the suspect to leave the home and not have contact with the child until the investigation is completed.

Some protocols, such as those developed in Tennessee by a state child sexual abuse task force with representatives from all involved disciplines, address the specifics of the investigative process. A similar model is offered by the National Child Advocacy Center in Huntsville, Alabama. These protocols not only outline the issues the team needs to address but also give direction on how to approach the issue in practice, including specific questions that must be answered (see Box 4.1).

Box 4.1: Protocol Concerns

Whether part of a formal investigative protocol approved at the senior management level or an informal protocol worked out by team members, at a minimum the team's protocols should address the following:

receiving a report
notifying the team
investigative decision making
location of interviews
parental notification
order of interviews
medical examinations
crime scene
validation decision making
case action decision making
court preparation

❏ Receiving the Report

Because the report may come into any one of several agencies, it is important that all members understand the kind of information needed up front by other team members. In most communities, the majority of reports are likely to come to CPS. If that is the case, then it is important that the CPS intake staff is sensitive to the needs of law enforcement, gathering any information from the referent that law enforcement personnel will need from the person making the report. There will be many common needs such as the child's name, date of birth, age, address, the location of the alleged victim, the child's parents' or caretaker's name and address, the reason why the report is being made, the type and circumstances of alleged abuse, where the abuse is alleged to have occurred, how long has it gone on, how the reporter knows of this situation, who else has knowledge, the name of the person the reporter believes is responsible for the abuse, and whether the alleged perpetrator has current access to the child. In addition to these general questions, law enforcement may have specific areas it wishes explored, including such details as the presence of physical evidence or witnesses to the abuse. The involved agencies should then check agency records for past history.

NOTIFICATION OF THE TEAM

The team needs to decide who wants to know about referrals and when. There may be cases in which all team members want immediate notification (i.e., homicides), while it may be more common that only the field investigative staff (CPS and law enforcement) will need to know right away.

❑ Investigative Decision Making

The team needs to have a process in place for such decisions as when to make the first contact, who will take the lead in which interviews, and how information will be shared with team members not present at the interviews. Decisions about audio- or videotaping need to be made early in the investigation. Absolutes of taping all or taping none of the interviews make this clear, but if the team is to decide this issue on a case-by-case basis, then a clear decision-making process needs to be in place.

LOCATION OF INTERVIEWS

Choosing the location of the interview with the child is important, and it is often recommended that it occur in a neutral environment. Some researchers suggest that this reduces the offender's psychological "power." Others have argued that the child's recall of events will be stimulated if interviewed in the location where the abuse is alleged to have occurred. The team needs to decide in which direction it wants to go.

Some teams rely heavily on interviews at the child's school, where the child feels comfortable and where the alleged offender has minimal power. A survey of teams in Tennessee found that 60% frequently used schools for this purpose (Tennessee Network for Child Advocacy, 1990). If the team chooses this option, then it must work out arrangements with school officials on the best time (e.g., an interview started 15 minutes before buses begin loading would not work well) and who will be involved in the interview (e.g., this site becomes far less attractive if the principal insists on and is allowed to sit in on the interview). At least one state (Tennessee) secured an attorney general's opinion to establish the team's right to interview in schools and developed a protocol with education officials to control who is present in the interviews. Certainly, on a local basis, it would be wise to work out these arrangements early on. In this way, the schools can identify staff members to facilitate the interviews more discretely.

When a team uses the school as an interview site, it must keep a low profile. Children are extremely sensitive to peer comments, and announcing to the entire student body what is happening does not encourage cooperation. Officers should arrive in unmarked cars and plain clothes. The school may also hold useful records about the child or have knowledge of the family.

The team must keep a low profile at school interview sites.

Other teams rely on a Child Advocacy Center or similar facility. These sites can be made quite child friendly and yet be equipped with audio- and videorecording capacity. In these situations, the team must consider how the child will be transported to the center and by whom. If no other option exists to conducting an interview where the abuse is believed to have occurred, then choose a location that deemphasizes the power of the alleged perpetrator and provides a degree of privacy so that the child will be as comfortable as possible in talking.

PARENT NOTIFICATION

Regardless of where the interview is conducted, the team must decide how and by whom parents will be notified of the interview. Prior notification would generally be preferred by parents, but to do so may result in a perpetrating parent influencing the child's statement. In other cases, the notification may result in the family fleeing the community or simply refusing to let investigators talk to the child. If the team opts for interviewing the child before parental notification, then it is still important that the team determine who will later explain the team's action to the parent(s). If the decision is made to interview the child at an advocacy center or similar location, then the team needs to be sure that it has the legal authority to transport the child to the site or it will have to rely on the parents to do so even with all of the associated adverse consequences.

ORDER OF INTERVIEWS

The team must decide in which order it will interview the principal actors. The Tennessee protocol, for example, suggests interviewing the child first to get his or her statement with a minimum of outside influence. Other protocols suggest talking with nonoffending parents first to gain information on what they know of the abuse, as well as background on the child, including likes and dislikes (e.g. foods, activities, television shows), daily routine and other relevant data (contact with the alleged offender, missing articles of clothing, notable behavioral changes). To do so, of course, one must weigh the danger of the parent "contaminating" the child's statement before investigators can meet with the child or of the parent warning the alleged offender. These are not idle concerns. Even the best intentioned parent will find it extremely difficult not to question a loved

Parents will find it extremely difficult not to question a loved child.

child about the possibility of abuse if afforded an opportunity. This questioning is just as much an "interview" as any done by a well-trained professional. It can also alter subsequent statements.

Decisions need to be made about when to interview other children, any witnesses or collateral contacts, the nonoffending parent(s), and the alleged perpetrator. In the Tennessee protocol, the alleged offender is the last to be interviewed, with the weight of all the evidence gathered used to encourage an admission. Other jurisdictions have had success confronting the alleged offender shortly after the child's interview, using surprise to help gain a confession (R. Cage, personal communication, 1991). Investigative protocols often address specific topics to be covered in the interviews and in some cases how to ask the questions.

MEDICAL EXAMINATION

The protocol should address when medical examinations will be required. Allegations of vaginal penetration clearly dictate a medical exam. Year-old allegations of fondling involving a 16-year-old female who denies that the incident occurred and is strongly opposed to an examination present the team with a dilemma. She may be trying to hide long-standing abuse or she may be forthright in her denials and would find a forced vaginal exam abusive in its own right. The protocol also should include who will conduct the medical exams in the community (qualifications, selected facilities, parental choice, etc.). Issues of how any evidence acquired through the exam will be secured and maintained also must be covered.

CRIME SCENE

The team needs to establish procedures for deciding when to seek a consent to search or a search warrant. Although CPS is not directly involved in search and seizure, it is important that it understand the rules of procedure in this area so as to be alert to possible objects that should be listed in the search warrant and sought by law enforcement. In brief, the following rules of evidence should be followed: proper recording of potential physical evidence; proper collection, containment, and marking of evidence; and following an appropriate chain of custody on the evidence. In the past, many law enforcement agencies gave intrafamilial child sexual abuse crime scenes little attention. It was felt in cases of intrafamilial abuse that the crime scene would have little to offer that would contribute substantially to the investigation. Having a suspect and victim living in the same quarters seemed to eliminate the opportunity to collect the types of physical evidence that most officers were used to looking for; for example, fingerprints in a bedroom where all members of the household have access greatly negates the significance of any latent prints recovered by processing the bedpost. With extrafamilial cases, the track record was a little bit better, in part because it was not perceived as a "real crime." Today we recognize that all crime scenes should be thoroughly examined if possible.

VALIDATION DECISION MAKING

Once all evidence has been gathered, the team needs to have an agreed on method of decision making on whether members believe the child was abused and, if so, by whom. This process, called *validation* in some states, pulls all the evidence together, including that which supports and refutes the allegation. The team needs to decide at the outset how this evidence will be weighed. These issues are discussed in Chapter 10 and by such authors as Faller.

CASE ACTION DECISION MAKING

If the team concludes that the abuse occurred, then it opens up a series of decisions that are the prime responsibility of usually one of the team's member agencies. This includes risk assessment and judgments about foster care by the child protection staff. The prosecutor and law enforcement officials have decisions to make about whether prosecution is indicated and, if so, how to proceed with charges. Decisions about treatment for the victim and perhaps the family need to be made. The protocol needs to outline the team's involvement in these decisions and how that interaction will occur.

COURT PREPARATION

The protocol needs to discuss any role the team will have in preparing the child and perhaps family for court.

By thinking through these issues and others unique to the local community, the team can reduce conflict and improve its effectiveness. When members know what to expect of one another and the general flow of the investigation, the team can focus on the case at hand rather than negotiating the process every time. The standard protocol, however, should not be treated as an inviolate policy. The team must be free to adjust the protocol to suit the unique features of individual cases as they arise.

5

Preparing for the Child Interview

Effective interviewing technique is part art, part learned skill, and part knowledgeable application of principles of psychology, child development, and human behavior. During a child abuse investigation, interviewers will have an opportunity to talk to people of all ages, in a variety of emotional states, and of possibly varying degrees of complicity with criminal activity. Professional investigators will work to develop skills that will enable them to expand their abilities to communicate in the most effective manner.

We already have discussed in general the decision-making process regarding who on the team should participate in the child victim interview(s). Although this decision is one of the most important the team will make, several other facets of the interview process need consideration.

The child victim is often the focal point of the investigation. The majority of sexual abuse cases provide little or no recognized medical or uncovered physical evidence, so the investigators must rely heavily on child interviews. Therefore, good, comprehensive child interviews are the cornerstone of these investigations. The team should plan, as much as possible, to include incentives for constructive interviews.

❑ Who Should Be Involved?

In examining the issue as to the person or persons who will conduct the child interview, the team must decide whether it would be more productive to do a joint interview or to allow one investigator to conduct the questioning. Both styles of interviewing have merit. A joint interview is conducted by more than one member of the team, representing differing disciplines. This is usually law enforcement and child protective service members. Joint interviews allow both of the primary investigative team members to cover material that each discipline needs in a minimum number of child contacts. Although more than one interview will probably still be necessary to elicit the complete statement of what happened (Sorensen & Snow, 1991), it will alleviate much duplication of questioning and allow both parties to observe the child's affect as he or she relates information. Where two individuals witness the same information being given, they can cross-check their interpretations of the child's statements. Joint interviews also provide for greater ability to record the child's words accurately and to cover more thoroughly the necessary ground.

Joint interviewers can cross-check their interpretations of the child's statements.

But a joint interview does have drawbacks. The more people present during interviews, the more difficult it may be to establish rapport with the child, who also may find it more difficult to share sensitive or painful information. Just as adults who have problems usually select a private place and one person in which to confide, so might the child appreciate the ability to confide in one individual.

If the persons conducting the interview do not establish who will take the lead in the questioning and how both parties will conduct the session, the interview can quickly degenerate into a volley of questions from both investigators without the child connecting with either person. In this environment, the child is not afforded the opportunity to respond fully to any inquiry. Noncoordinated investigators may each be following their own agenda with little regard for the other professionals' needs or those of the child. Where the two have vastly differing interviewing styles (e.g., fast-paced and assertive versus more relaxed and nondirective), the child might become even more confused and threatened. Such interviews can be disastrous.

The team may decide to let one member conduct the interview with the child. This may be done while other professionals watch and listen unobserved by the child (e.g., as through a one-way mirror or closed circuit monitor). This method has the advantage of confronting the child with only one person with whom to establish rapport, one set of disclosures to worry about, and one set of job descriptions to understand. It does put an additional burden on the lone interviewer, who needs to ask questions covering both social work and law enforcement concerns. Unless there is the technological ability to get immediate feedback and prompting from observers (e.g., through an earpiece radio receiver), cues from the child might be missed and not addressed, and other team members' special concerns might get short shift. This interviewer must be soundly grounded in legally acceptable interviewing techniques: establishing a proper foundation and understanding of the child's developmental level, ensuring that the child understands the importance of accuracy, and avoiding the undue use of leading questions. The interviewer must also know the needs of the other team members. Factors that influence the legal acceptability of interviews include the minimal use of "leading" questions that require only a "yes" or "no" response and the lack of clarifying questions to the child's responses. For example, the first situation is to be avoided is typified as follows:

Interviewer: Now, Krista, we are here today to talk with you about the report we got saying your teacher, Mr. Bill, has been putting his hand in your panties. Is that what he does?
Child: Uh huh.
Interviewer: Okay.

A better approach is as follows:

Interviewer: Now, Krista, do you know why we want to talk with
   you today?
Child: No.
Interviewer: We want to talk with you about stuff that happens at
   school. We talk with a lot of kids. Why don't we start by getting
   your teacher's name.

Yet another workable approach is this:

Interviewer: I understand your teacher's name is Mr. Bill.
Child: Yeah.
Interviewer: Tell us about him. What does he look like?

Another drawback to the solo interviewer comes when the child,
for whatever reason, does not feel comfortable with the interviewer;
there is no obvious alternative for the child. He or she may decide
not to share what has happened rather than talk with this person. In
a joint interview, the child readily sees the option of focusing on one
or the other interviewer.

In the solo interview, any defense challenge to the questions or
methodology falls on one person. The joint interview affords an
opportunity for immediate intervention if less-than-acceptable techniques are used, without compromising the entire interview.

The most significant drawback of the solo interview is its potential
to undermine the basic team concept. Although both investigative
members of the team initially respond to calls and may jointly make
the decision for only one of them to talk to the child, after a period
of time it can become routine and too easy to place the responsibility
of most child interviews on one team member with instructions to
"Call me if you get anything." The process then changes to one of
triage, in which the team investigation begins only after one person
has made the decision that his or her interview contained actionable
material.

❏ The Role of Authority in the Interview

For law enforcement team members, additional precautions before the child interviews are advisable. The interviewers will introduce themselves to the child. The introduction will contain their names and occupations. The law enforcement officer *must* make clear to the child that the child is *not* in trouble and that the officer's role is *not* to arrest the child. This cannot be overemphasized.

Many parents, even law abiding ones, may have inadvertently portrayed the police officers seen in daily life as individuals who only arrest people and put them in jail. The parents may even have threatened the child in jest or frustration with police intervention at some point. This problem is far greater if the child lives in a household or community in which he or she has observed family members or friends placed under arrest. Preadolescents and teens may have had their own scrapes with law enforcement officers. All of these factors may generate fear of the officer.

In preparing to interview children, all interviewers must take time to work out an explanation for their roles as investigators. This explanation should emphasize their place as "helpers" who are there for the child's best interest. With young children, this can be a short piece; for older children, it may involve several minutes of description, with the child asking clarifying questions. The following situation exemplifies this approach:

Officer: Hello. My name is Donna Pence. You may call me Donna. What's your name?

Child: Kathy.

Officer: Well, Kathy, we're going to spend some time talking together today. I like to get to know the children I talk to and I like for them to get to know me. I'm a police officer. Have you ever met a police officer before?

Child: No.

Officer: Do you know what a police officer's job is?

Child: To arrest bad people and put them in jail.

Officer: You're partly right. Some officers do that. But my job is a little bit different. My job is to talk to kids. That is just about all I do. I talk to kids about different things—things that make them

happy, things that make them sad and glad; things that they do
and things that they do with other people. Part of my job is also
to try and help children who have problems. Do you understand
all that?

Child: Yes.

Officer: Do you have any questions about my job?

Child: Do you have a badge and carry a gun like police on TV?

Officer: Yes, I do. Would you like to see my badge?

Child: Uh huh. Can I touch it?

Officer: Sure you can.

The preparation for an officer should include a realistic appraisal
of how children will view them. It is recommended that officers wear
plain clothes when conducting interviews. The uniform may have
either a positive or negative impact on the interview, depending on
the child's age, gender, or background. It is better to avoid this
impact altogether, if possible.

We believe that *no officer should ever carry a firearm into the child
interview* when it can be avoided. The weapon is often a distraction
that may cause fear on the part of children or simply divert their
attention as they try to get the officer to allow them to handle it. The
mere presence of the weapon could be cited by the defense as a
theoretical source of intimidation used by the police to coerce an
alleged false statement.

A child can respond very favorably to law enforcement presence.
The officer represents safety and authority. This might well enable a
fearful child to open up, feeling that the power of the offender has
been blunted or negated by the implied power of the officer.

The social counselor, too, must be prepared to explain his or her
role. The possibility of previous contacts with the child's family
could affect the child's' ability to see a social counselor as a "helper"
as opposed to a "meddler." This may be particularly true if the child
has had previous foster care placements. In some communities, these
counselors are perceived to be disruptive to the family, rather than
protective or unifying. The very power that the worker has to protect
the child (that is, removal from the household) may be the very thing
that the child is afraid will happen if he or she discloses. Few children

would welcome the idea of being taken away from everything that is familiar, including toys, clothes, friends, school, and pets.

❑ Documenting the Interview

A decision the team must make before any interview is how to document the child interviews. Unlike most interviews with adults, much baggage has been attached to children's statements. Research on children's suggestibility, interviewers' ability to "lead" them, and misinterpretation of information given by children to adults (Ceci, Toglia, & Ross, 1987; Faller, 1992; Goodman & Aman, 1987; Goodman & Clarke-Stewart, 1991; Saywitz, Goodman, Nichols, & Moran, 1991) has prompted a groundswell response to make sure that the children are questioned in an age-appropriate, nonleading, and objective manner. These interviews and the methods of eliciting information are closely scrutinized. For this reason, the issue of how best to memorialize the child interview has been debated far and wide.

Accurate documentation of these interviews is extremely important. The team can conduct an excellent interview and elicit accurate data, but if the information gained is not documented in an acceptable format, then the end result in any subsequent legal forums will be almost as if the interview had not taken place. If this happens, then the children in need of protection may be exposed to continued abuse because of poor documentation. All of us know what it is like to be overwhelmed with cases and go from one child interview to another without having

Accurate documentation of these interviews is extremely important.

time to really reflect on what was said until a week later when we try to catch up on our paperwork. Trying to recall the exact questions and answers plus the child's affect is extremely difficult, if not impossible, under these conditions. Yet judicial systems that must decide what is in children's best interests will expect interviewers to do exactly that. Three methods of memorializing information given by children have been used and discussed: written reports, audio-taped statements, and videotaped statements.

❏ Written Reports

The written report is a time-tested way to record information that has been used by all disciplines. It is familiar to all involved, including the school-aged child. Although it has the advantage of the familiar, it is sometimes difficult to use effectively in this type of interview. For the solo interviewer to ask and record questions, watch the child give responses, and record the responses exactly as the child gave them, as well as to think ahead to what should be asked next, is impossible. A joint interview setting offers more flexibility, because the support interviewer can write while the lead interviewer asks the questions. In either case, the ensuing document will be challenged on the grounds that even the person(s) conducting the interview do not know the accuracy of the information contained within. Cases have been encountered in which the written report describes a dramatic disclosure in response to excellently phrased questions. In one such situation, the problem was that further investigation on the case determined the interviewer routinely did not conduct interviews as described in reports. In fact, the interviewer had weak skills but knew how it should be done and reported accordingly.

The very drawbacks that make written case summaries weak also make them desirable in the eyes of some prosecutors. It is more difficult for a defense attorney to challenge exactly what questions were asked and how they were presented if this information is inexact in the report. The jury must then choose whose recollections to believe.

❏ Audiotaped Statements

Many agencies have recorded statements on audiotapes for years. It has been a fast, relatively cheap, and easy way to document encounters. With the unobtrusiveness of newer models of recorders and the higher quality of available equipment, it has become the method of choice for many teams. It gives investigators the advantage of being able to devote their full attention to the child being interviewed without having to stop the child in midnarration to make sure they are writing every word down or to slow the child as he or she really begins to relate events.

Three issues cause problems here. First, how capable is the equipment and how competent is the operator? Does the recorder work? Are the batteries strong? Is there enough tape? Is the microphone sensitive enough to pick up a child's soft voice? Does its presence inhibit the child? Does its use distract the child? Does the interviewer feel comfortable using it? Can tapes be changed without fuss?

The second issue has to do with dimension. A written report is a one-dimensional representation of the interview. Those reading it get a "feel" for the child only by the words on the page. An audio-taped statement takes this one step further and allows reviewers to hear the child. We can note hesitations, inflections, distress, and emotions. This may have a direct bearing on how listeners act or react to the report of abuse. It may well make a difference in keeping a case open when the child says, "No, this didn't happen to me" but his or her voice is full of pain or otherwise contradicts the words.

The third issue has to do with "housekeeping": Who keeps the tape? Under what conditions? Who decides on making copies? For what purpose? Who has the authority to review? This tape is a piece of evidence and is subject to chain of custody and security, as is any other form of evidence. Even if the tape is unintelligible, it must be maintained and not destroyed or otherwise taped over. Defense attorneys also will be able to listen to every "I don't know," "I don't remember," and "No, it didn't happen," and they will perhaps question every inquiry from the interviewer's mouth in an attempt to discredit the statements' content.

❏ Videotaped Statements

The practice of videotaping deserves careful review. In the mid-1980s, videotaping child interviews was hailed as the way to resolve all problems with child interviewing. Many states passed laws that allowed the use of videotapes in investigations or litigation. Different local departments and agencies had a variety of experiences with videotaping. As a result, some no longer use such taping, and in some jurisdictions prosecutors adamantly oppose it. As with other forms of documentation, there are advantages and disadvantages in videotaping. It may reduce the number of times a child is questioned or the number of interviewers who feel that they must talk with the child; it provides the most complete documentation of what is said to the child and how the child responds both orally and physically. This gives the third dimension—sight—to the child interview for other reviewers. What is the child's body language? Does the child's affect match his or her statements? Seeing distress or elation as the child describes some activity is important in the decision-making process. Having the interview videotaped may document that proper interview techniques were used and consequently reduce challenges. The tape can be used to persuade a nonoffending parent of the victimization or the offender to admit to his or her actions and enhance the probability of a later guilty plea. The tape can be used with the victim to refresh memory in court preparation or it can substitute for the child's testimony in some legal settings.

Reviewing videotapes is also one method by which investigators can critically evaluate their techniques and improve. They can check to see that all areas of the statement were fully covered, that nothing was missed or omitted, and that no loose ends need follow-up investigation or clarification. Supervisors may use the tapes to review specific cases when a consultation is deemed necessary or for general performance evaluations.

But one other important reason for videotaping is this:

> Experienced child abuse investigators and prosecutors know that children have their own unique vocabulary when describing incidents of molestation. The metaphors and analogies of children are unlike those of adults, and it is imperative that they be reported accurately. Further, in several months or years between initial disclosure and trial, tremendous developmental changes can occur with the child. It is extremely helpful for the jury to see or hear the child, through videotape, closer in time to the abuse. (Stephenson, 1992, p. 6)

The disadvantages of videotaping have come to light over the last few years. Some of these drawbacks are also associated with audio recording. Prosecuting attorney Paul Stern (1992) has articulated the following drawbacks to videotaping:

- The in-court use of a single videotaped interview is exceptionally misleading. The investigative interview with the child is merely one point along this continuum of disclosure. As such, it represents just a single snapshot in time and will possibly be given greater weight than any other out-of-court statement the child has given. To have one isolated interview reproducible before a jury is to encourage the jury to place exaggerated and unwarranted importance on that one piece of evidence.
- Videotaped interviews presented to a jury allow the defense to change the focus of the trial away from the child's answers and onto the interviewer's questions. There is no perfect interview, no agreement on a specific protocol for investigative interviews, and therefore a defense attorney will seek to make counsel's own protocol the jury's protocol and measure the videotaped interview against it.
- The knowledge that a particular interview is being videotaped can increase the pressure on the child and decrease the fluidity of disclosure.
- A technical or administrative error can have devastating results. In some states, destruction of evidence, even if unintentional, can require dismissal of a charge.

If the decision is made by the team to videotape child interviews, it triggers several needs:

1. accessibility of equipment
2. location suitable for videotaping
3. training for those who will be operating the equipment
4. development of protocols for use of the videotaping
5. training for interviewers to increase their on-camera comfort level
6. protocols for decision making as to where the videotaped interview(s) will be housed, under what conditions it will be shown, and whether copies will be made and how they will be protected (Home Office, 1992; Myers, 1992)

The team also needs to keep in mind that in some cases videotaping will have been a part of the abuse, and great sensitivity needs to be exercised in deciding how to document the interview.

In some jurisdictions in which videotaping is not acceptable, child interviews frequently are audiotaped. We fail to understand why this occurs. Audiotapes have the same disadvantages as videotapes but lack the compelling visual element.

The issue of documenting is not merely one of recording information but also one of processing and disseminating the fruits of the interview. Whose agency transcribes the interviews, makes copies of them, and distributes them to the team are all areas that can cause team conflict. It needs to be clearly articulated how the paperwork will be handled. On taped interviews that are typed from the tapes, checking the transcripts for accuracy is absolutely necessary. It also may be necessary for the interviewer to review the transcript and fill in the inaudible moments that usually are present. With younger children, in particular, it may be difficult for support staff members to understand the child's words, whereas the actual interviewer may well have a vivid recollection of the exact words used.

❑ Interview Aids

Irrespective of who conducts the interview or where it is to be held, each individual interviewer should review the variety of interviewing aids available, receive training on how best to use them, and decide, with input from other team members, which ones to use in the investigative interview setting. Different aids (e.g., dolls, drawings, puppets) have been designed for specific purposes for different disciplines. Some useful tools were not designed for this purpose at all and yet can work well. There are aids that work with one gender or age group better than others. All of these must be considered before their use in an interview. Some older children may need nothing more than a listening ear paying attention just to them. The wise team will research first what items are acceptable by prosecutors and local courts as well as what the budget will bear. Many teams have found local groups that are willing to make or purchase items the team needs.

DOLLS

Aside from the child-sized furniture to go in any prepared interview room, the most common interviewing aid mentioned is the anatomically detailed doll. These dolls are available in different races, genders, and ages for use in different cases. This aid can be valuable for the child who is having difficulty describing what happened, or it can be used by the interviewer to clarify what the child has described. The dolls are not a panacea to ensure that every child will be able to show minute details as to what if anything happened, and they should not be used as such.

Any person using the dolls will benefit from training on their appropriate use. The team should either adopt the protocols that come with purchased dolls or develop its own. These protocols will ensure that the dolls are properly used, and they can guard against later defense attacks on their use in the interview setting.

Generally, the dolls are not used until the child has made an initial disclosure and needs the assistance of this communication tool. For example, a 6-year-old girl orally says her uncle put his penis "down there," but she is having difficulty explaining; the interviewer may ask her to show her with the dolls. With the dolls the child can demonstrate the interaction, and she may also find it easier to describe orally what she is doing. Some interviewers also use the dolls for body part identification. If that is done, the dolls should be dressed afterward and put away until needed again. The dolls are communication tools and should not be used diagnostically.

With the dolls the child can demonstrate the interaction.

Research on how sexually abused children interact with the dolls seems to show that their use in the sex abuse interview is *not* suggestive, despite defense claims to the contrary (Everson & Boat, 1990; Goodman & Aman, 1990). Our experience has been that girls and younger children tend to react better to the use of dolls. In general, older boys and adolescents do not feel comfortable with the dolls, but if the interviewer feels they must be used, it is best to remove them from sight as soon as they have served their purpose.

Some children do better with traditional dolls, such as the Hart Family™ or Barbie™ and Ken™. These are toys that are familiar to the children, and they may generate less anxiety. If the description of abuse is such that genital identification is necessary, then the anatomically detailed dolls can be introduced.

No matter what types of dolls are available, the team may find it beneficial to have several common changes of clothing available. Night attire or swimming gear may make it easier for the child who has being wearing this type of clothing before or during the activity to show how the abuse played itself out. These accessories may be purchased, but they might also be made by local sewing groups and donated to the team.

OTHER MEDIA

Conducting a developmental assessment is a normal part of all child interviews. There is equipment designed for this specific purpose, but interviewers can use simple cards or books, which are inexpensive and available at school supply houses or toy stores. Anything that has colors, numbers, and types of familiar animals or characters can be used.

Hand puppets also can be useful in interviewing. Children may find it less threatening to talk to or through a puppet. These can be inexpensive knitted socks or the more elaborate animal puppets. If animal puppets are used, then the interviewer must be sensitive to possible fears, such as those of spiders or snakes. Investigators also need to be alert to the possibility that the child may enter into the fantasy realm with the puppets, thus potentially neutralizing the acceptance of the reliability of any subsequent child disclosures.

Children can use dollhouses to show family activity or the placement of individuals before, during, or after abusive events. Working in the dollhouse to show where people normally go may help to lead into an abuse disclosure. If a videotape is being made of the interview, the dollhouse selected should have no walls for ease of recording what the child is showing. Dollhouses should be equipped with all normal rooms, including bathrooms.

DRAWING

Perhaps the most important interviewing aids are the simplest: paper and markers. As a whole, children love to draw, and this is an excellent communication tool (E. Amacher, personal communication, 1985). Again, we are not using their art for diagnostic purposes but to assist the child in relaying accurate information to us. It is generally the oral explanation that accompanies the art that is most important. In the beginning of the interview, art also can be used in developmental assessment. If and when the child begins to describe an abusive situation, he or she can draw segments of the abuse that can assist the team in validating the child's statement. Some of these drawings are quite powerful. Children can draw pictures of instrumentalities of the crime, floor plans of the locations of abuse, and body parts. Children can list classmates or other children who may be victims or witnesses. Markers are sometimes perceived by children as better than crayons because they do not break, melt, or look used as quickly.

Whatever interview aids are used, proper documentation of what was used, when, and why is needed. Any artwork the child created should be treated as adjuncts to the interview and marked and retained as evidence.

Material that is designed for sex abuse prevention or treatment should not be used early in the investigative interview. This opens the interviewer to accusations that it was really the programmed materials rather than the child's experience that led the child to the sexual discussion.

When the team has considered who will actually conduct the interview, how it will be documented, and which tools are likely to facilitate an accurate statement from the child, the team is ready to move to the next step.

6

The Child Interview Process

The child interview is the cornerstone of the investigation. The interviewer's communication skills must include knowledge of children's cognitive and language development.

The first *investigative* interview is distinct from the first interview. All investigators must remember that if the child has intentionally disclosed, then he or she has talked to at least one person (perhaps the person who made the referral) and probably more. How many times has the child been interviewed by untrained, yet concerned, individuals such as parents, teachers, friends, and others? How have these conversations affected the child and the information that the child will or will not be sharing with the interviewer? Has any nonbelieving person or the alleged offender tried to discourage the disclosure (Cage, 1991)?

> *The child interview is the cornerstone of the investigation.*

The information given by the child should be considered a *statement* and always referred to as such. This is the term we regularly use in talking about information shared by adults, even defendants. By not using the same terminology for children, we give the impression that what the child has told us should be given less weight than what an adult has told us. The word that has traditionally been used—*story*—has connotations of fabrication. Webster's *New World Dictionary* defines *story* as "the telling of an event or series of events, whether true or fictitious; account; narration; . . . a report or rumor; a falsehood or fib."

The interviewer must be prepared to speak to the child in developmentally appropriate language. The choice of words, sentence structure, and simple nature of the questions will be critical in ensuring that the child understands what is being asked. This is one of the most important and yet most overlooked aspects of investigative interviewing of children, especially young children.

> Children's apparent lack of credibility has as much to do with the competence of adults to relate to and communicate with children as it does with children's abilities to remember and relate their experience accurately. (Karen Saywitz, quoted in Saywitz & Nathanson, 1993, p. 3)

The same principles apply to the interpretation of what the child says. For example, asking a 3-year-old a simple question such as, "Who hurt you—your brother or the teacher?" might lead to confusion when the child repeats the word "teacher" because he or she does not understand the concept of "or." One must always be cautious in interpreting a child's statement. *Responsive listening*—in which the interviewer repeats to the child what the child has just said—is an important technique for reducing the risk that the interviewer will misconstrue what the child actually said or meant. Undoubtedly, adults tend to relate to and interpret what children say from their own adult perspective, and often questions posed by adults are misconstrued by children. For example:

Adult: How did you sleep last night?
Child (3 years, 8 months of age): In my bed.

Team members must educate themselves about children's cognitive and language development. The available literature includes

---
Team members
must educate
themselves about
child development.
---

material originally intended for day care teachers (Braga & Braga, 1975), child abuse-specific literature (MacFarlane & Waterman, 1986), and language development (Clark & Clark, 1977; Walker, 1992). The team can also find natural laboratories by simply visiting day care centers and talking with children in general about what they think is important.

Those who deal with children must remember these two general categories of language: *receptive,* or words that are understood by the listener, and *expressive,* or words that are used by the speaker. As Joe and Laurie Braga (1975) point out in *Learning and Growing: A Guide to Child Development,* children use language even before they master its meaning, often producing speechlike sounds that they use to refer to objects but only with physical gestures that convey actual intent. First words usually begin around the first year. By approximately 20 months of age, children have some 50 single words in their vocabulary, and they may begin to put words together to form phrases. They cannot consistently answer why, when, or how questions until 5 or 6 years old (Steward, Bussey, Goodman, & Saywitz, 1993). As they develop, so does their ability to communicate their needs, wants, and descriptions of what is happening in their lives. We must recognize that small children may grasp many things that they do not yet have words for and that they know (and sometimes frequently use) words they do not really understand. This also applies to older children. For example:

Parent: Lucy, how long is it going to take us to get to New York?
Child (3 years, 8 months): (holds up three fingers)
Parent: Three hours?
Child: Minutes.

The child relates the question to the general category of time and is aware of time words. Her usage in this instance is "correct" in that she comprehends that she is being asked a time question. Her response also illustrates, however, that even though she knows *minute* is a unit of time, she does not have any idea of the length of a minute. Also note that she held up three fingers, indicating that she understands that numerals are associated with time. We would speculate that the number three may have been chosen because of its significance for her: It is her age.

Understanding and comprehension of time and number questions is extremely important in most of our cases, and interviewers, as part of the preinterview developmental assessment, should explore the child's level of accuracy in these areas. The interviewer might ask the child to explain terms such as *next, then, after, before, tomorrow, yesterday,* and *last* (Deitrich-MacLean, 1991). Asking the child to count from 1 to 10 or 20 and then count the number of objects in a group (e.g., 5 birds on a flash card) can check the child's ability to translate the abstract, rote counting process to a concrete example. Although it may not definitely assure the interviewer that the child is completely accurate when she says she was touched "five" times, if she can show that she can neither count to 5 nor identify 5 items (the birds on the card), then the interviewer should be leery of accepting the accuracy of a child's statement that she was molested precisely five times.

❑ Developmental Considerations

In a review of the current literature on child development and its implications for interviewing children, Steward, Bussey, Goodman, and Saywitz (1993) make the following observations:

- Children's ability to communicate accurately is enhanced when tasks are grounded in real-life experiences (e.g., home routine on a typical day).
- Children's ability is enhanced when there are experiences that are personally significant or emotionally salient for them.
- Young children can be logical about simple events that have meaning for their lives.
- Young children can accurately recall routine events that they have experienced.

- If complex events can be broken into simple, more manageable units, then children's accounts of them can be expected to improve (e.g., such questions that determine routines in the home can be used: Who wakes you up in the morning? Who picks out your clothes? Who helps you get dressed? What do you have for breakfast? Who fixes your breakfast?).

- Children rely on context and clues, so younger children often need more support for their memories in the way of external reminders of events (e.g., to frame the time of suspected abuse, such questions can be used as, Do you remember your birthday? What kind of birthday cake did you have? Did you get any presents? What did you get?).

- The more peripheral the detail, the poorer the memories of both children and adults.

- Even memory for events that are personally significant to children become less detailed over time.

- Most children are quite accurate in their *free recall* of events (answers to questions such as, What happened?).

- The use of suggestive questioning can lead to errors in children's reports, but it is easier to elicit errors with peripheral details than with personally significant events.

- Direct or even leading questions may sometimes be necessary to elicit embarrassing, poorly remembered, or secretive information from children. For example, consider the interview of a 12-year-old boy about the underwear kept by the offender after the abuse:

Interviewer: After visiting Gene, did he ever keep anything of yours?

Child: Nope.

Interviewer: Did he ever ask you to give him anything of yours?

Child: Nope.

Interviewer: Did he ever keep any of your clothing?

Child: (Pause) No, I don't remember. . . .

Interviewer: What about your underwear?

Child: (Long pause; averts reddened face from female interviewer) Oh . . . one time after we went camping I couldn't find it, but just one time.

- Experimental work has demonstrated that children as young as 4 years of age know the difference between telling the truth and telling a lie. They also know it is wrong to lie.

- As children mature, they learn that telling the truth can get them into trouble.

❏ Starting the Interview

If a video or audio recording is made, we recommend that it be operating from the time the child enters the room. The person who escorts the child into the room should introduce the officer and the child protective service worker. The introduction is brief but is constructed in a way that assists in relaxing the child. If appropriate to the child's age, the interviewers may shake hands with her and offer her a place to sit. (*Note:* The female gender will be used throughout with the understanding that males are also included.) They also sit and become comfortable, perhaps with younger children all sitting on the floor. Not ignoring the child's comfort, the lead interviewer asks about her, perhaps telling her that it is all right to remove her shoes (again, if age-appropriate) or otherwise do what is necessary to relax. If appropriate, an interviewer might also ask if the child would like juice or soda. If the interviewer is going to drink coffee or Coke during the interview, then politeness would dictate offering the child something similar. (Ironically, even this simple courtesy may be attacked as a "blatant bribe" by some defense "expert.")

The *lead* interviewer confirms the child's identity and asks whether the child remembers the interviewers' names. If not, then the lead repeats the first names and begins the rapport-building and developmental assessment portion of the interview. The lead should explain his or her discipline's role, and then the *secondary* interviewer explains his or her discipline's role. The child is given the opportunity to ask clarifying questions on role explanations. The lead might choose at this point to explain the presence of any camera or tape recorder. For example:

Lead: Do you know what that is in the corner?
Child: Yes, it makes movies.
Lead: Have you ever seen one of them before?
Child: Uh huh. My dad has one.
Lead: Does he take pictures of you with it?
Child: Yeah, when I do something special like getting my Brownie patches.
Lead: Well, we use ours for something a little bit different. You see, Charles [the secondary interviewer] and I are pretty old and

have trouble remembering stuff sometimes. Our camera helps us remember what kids have told us. We talk to kids all the time and they tell us lots of things. All of it is important, so we want to be sure and get right who told us what. Is it okay with you if we do that today?

Child: Am I going to be on TV?

Lead: Just our TV. This does not show up in people's houses like a regular show. After we talk today, I'm going to take the tape and keep it in my office. The only people who will see it are the other people who help Charles and me.

Child: Okay.

Taking time to explain to the child the "rules of the game" can be important. Adults understand the interview process, and most know what is expected of them. Children do not. In their previous experience, when adults sit them down to talk, the child is in trouble. Having a stranger drop into her life and begin this same process is disconcerting and out of the norm. The interviewers must frame the experience for the child. By giving her a clear list of expectations, they make it easier for her to concentrate on what the interviewer is asking. The most common error in investigative interviewing is rushing the child. Go slowly to get the most accurate information. For example:

Lead: Alex, we are going to be asking you a lot of questions today. I want you to try and answer the ones you know the answer to. But this is not a test. If I ask you something and you don't know what the answer is, you can just tell me, "I don't know" and that is the right answer. When we're talking, I want us to talk about stuff that really happened. We don't talk about make believe or pretend. Please don't guess or, if you do, tell me it's a guess. Do you understand?

Child: Yeah.

Lead: Okay. Let's say I ask you what your mother's favorite color is. You don't know because she's never told you. But you see that she wears a lot of yellow and she wants to paint your room yellow. So what would you tell me her favorite color is?

Child: I don't know . . . but it might be yellow?

Lead: That's the right answer! Very good. Now sometimes I might use a word that you don't know what it means. If I do that, it's okay for you to say, "I don't know what that word is." I'll try to explain it or find an easier word. Okay?

Child: (Nods)

Lead: I might ask you a question that you know the answer to but have trouble talking about. If that happens, you just tell me and we'll try and figure out a way to make it easier for you. Okay?

Child: Okay.

Lead: After Charles and I finish asking you questions, we're going to give you a chance to ask us anything you want to know. Sometimes grown-ups talk to kids and don't give the kids a chance to talk back. We don't want to do that to you. And it's very important that if you say something and I say it back to you but I don't get it right, you tell me. Just because I'm a grown-up doesn't mean I am always right. We want to know what you said, not what we think you said. Okay?

By exploring the parameters of the interview in segments, it makes it easier for the child to understand and ask questions about any specific "rule" she does not understand. It also makes it easier for the interviewer to later remind the child of a rule if it seems the child is having difficulty with one of the concepts.

This area of the interview is part of trust and rapport building. If age-appropriate, the interviewer is treating the child as an equal in the process and giving the child control rather than allowing her to operate in the dark. In addition, it is part of the developmental assessment because the interviewer looks at the child's ability to comprehend the rules and the terms used by the questioner. Telling the child where the bathroom is and letting her know that a break at any time is okay can be empowering.

Depending on the child's age, the developmental assessment may take only a few questions or be comparatively long. Nevertheless, a proper assessment is critical so that the interviewer will be able to phrase questions in developmentally appropriate language and the team will be able to assess better the child's understanding of events in her life. How a young child uses and understands prepositions (*on, off, over, under, in, out,* etc.), for example, will be extremely important should the child describe activity in which clothes are on or off or when hands were in or out of clothing.

The interviewer also checks both expressive and receptive language levels. Using animal flash cards to look at the child's level of everyday comprehension can be an easy way to start this process with preschool children. For example:

Lead: Lucy, I have some cards we can play a game with. Okay?
Child: Okay.
Lead: When I show you a card, you can tell me what is on it and we'll put it down over here. Can you tell me what this number is?
Child: One.
Lead: Very good. What is this a picture of?
Child: Doggie.
Lead: What color is the doggie?
Child: Brownie.
Lead: Right again. You can put the card on the floor. What is the number on this card?
Child: Two!
Lead: Good. And what picture is here?
Child: Bird.
Lead: And what does a bird say?
Child: Tweet tweet.
Lead: What color is the bird?
Child: Bird is blue.
Lead: What is the bird sitting in?
Child: His nest.
Lead: What is the nest on?
Child: Big tree.
Lead: Do you have trees at your house?
Child: Yeah.
Lead: Are they big trees or little trees?

Frequently, in an attempt to avoid the appearance of leading the child, interviewers will ask choice questions using the word *or*. If children do not understand that they are being offered a choice or for some other reason do not understand the question, they often give a response that bears no relation to the question or they repeat back to the interviewer the last words of the selection. Children also may choose the answer to which they have some relationship, such as the 2-year-old child presented with a dual abstract choice. For example:

Adult: Allie, are you two smart or ten smart?
Child: (Considering) Te . . . Two!
Adult: Two smart?
Child: Yes. I two years old.

The barriers of language and the varying meanings of words are exacerbated when the interviewer interacts with a child from a different ethnic or racial group. Some children will speak a completely different language such as Spanish. At other times, English words will have different meanings. For example, a child on the Three Feathers Reservation in Oklahoma might describe a nonrelative as "grandfather" because all elders in the tribe are considered grandfather (Dobrec, 1992). On learning that the individual whom he or she thought was the child's grandparent is not related, an investigator might decide that the child simply does not developmentally understand the questions being asked. In reality, it is the investigator who does not understand.

The developmental assessment phase also looks at how the child communicates, what types of questions she can reliably answer, what helps her remember, and how she interacts with interviewers. One suggestion for doing this involves asking the child to describe a familiar experience, such as going to the grocery store. This exchange can provide interviewers with the basis for determining the child's skill in remembering the past and the level of assistance the interviewers must provide to facilitate the child's recall (Deitrich-MacLean, 1991). Listen for the types of errors the child makes. Are they errors in which the child adds something (an error of commission) or leaves something out (an error of omission)? Children are more likely to make errors of omission than commission (Steward et al., 1993).

Whether the child is African American, Latino, or any other background, the team must be prepared to adjust to meet the child's needs. This pursuit of cultural competence can lead to specialized reading, training, or consultation. In areas of the Southeast and Midwest, where a vast majority of the population falls into only two general racial groups, the team can prepare better through training and experience to cross-cultural language barriers. In other, more ethnically diverse communities, the challenge is far greater.

With this in mind, the developmental assessment and rapport building can go hand in hand. During this segment the interviewer is also asking questions about the child and her background. These include school, grade, teacher information, favorite and least liked subjects, and favorite foods. At this point, the interviewer is keeping to fairly neutral topics but can work toward a key question such as, "Do you know why you're here today?" If the child answers in the affirmative, the interviewer can ask what the child believes. This may lead directly into the issue of abuse. The interviewer also needs to explore how and why the child gained information about the purpose of the interview. If another adult has told the child, then the issues of who and what was said can be important. If a parent told the child, the interviewer should also ask what this parent told the child to tell the interviewer. It may be as innocent as "Tell the truth," but it could be more problematic if the child was told specifics to share such as, "Daddy hurts my bottom."

Should the child reply that she does not know, the interviewer must introduce the topic of abuse. Many interviewers choose to start generally with a reminder of information shared early in the interview as to the job of the interviewers. Namely, we talk with children about the things that happen in their lives, things that make them happy, sad, mad, upset, and so on. Comments such as, "We understand that some things may have happened at home [school, church, Scouts, day care] that you have not liked [asked questions about, had concerns over, is a bit unusual]," can be excellent openers. Using terms such as *hurt, bad,* and *abuse* should be avoided. Some of the behaviors of offenders do not cause pain but may well cause confusion on the part of the child. Specifically asking about *hurt* may elicit no information from concrete-thinking youngsters who have felt no pain. Use of judgmental terms are extremely dangerous. Initially, interviewers do not know the extent of the abuse and how involved the offender has been with the child. If the abuse has advanced to the point in which the child is not only a victim but also a participant in abusing other children, then she is not likely to disclose to people who tell her this behavior is "bad."

Whatever opener is selected, it should be general and not sex abuse-specific. For this reason, any interviewing aids used at this point should likewise be general in nature and contain no abuse-specific information. The interviewers want the information to come from the child; they should do their best not to let the child know what she believes they "want" or "need" to hear. Children may try to please an interviewer if they have some idea of what is being sought just to draw the interview to an end. Several experts in the field have recommended that the interview move from general questions to more specific questioning and then to abuse-specific questions. If the child describes an abusive situation, then the interviewer should get *complete* details of one episode before moving on to ask, "What happened next?" or "Did it ever happen before?" If the child is describing an event in a narrative fashion, then let the child finish before asking any needed clarifying questions. Then move the child into the next episode. One of the most frustrating things to encounter, in an otherwise good interview, is a passage such as follows:

Lead: When you were camping, where did you sleep?
Child: In David's tent.
Lead: What happened that night?
Child: He touched my private.
Lead: And then what happened?
Child: He wanted me to touch his private.
Lead: What did you do?
Child: I told him no.
Lead: Then what happened?
Child: The next day he tried to touch me again when we went for a swim.

In this interview section, the interviewer has moved so swiftly that it is difficult to draw conclusions based on the information provided. There is no detail, beginning, or ending to either episode mentioned. How did the child end up sharing the tent with David? Who *is* David? Is this the first time they have shared a tent? Were they in sleeping bags? The same bag? What was David wearing? What was the child wearing? Was the touching above or beneath the clothing? What did David say before, during, and after the event? How did

David indicate he wanted the child to touch his body? What did the child hear while David was touching her underneath her clothing? The details of each episode should be covered as completely as possible before moving on, because each event is a separate criminal charge, and each needs complete details.

To establish venue, the interviewer should also ask (unless otherwise obvious) if the child knows the actual location where the abuse occurred. If the possibility of out-of-state travel exists, then confirmation by the child, parent(s), or neutral adult witness may lead to federal criminal charges in addition to state charges. Given the frequency with which children describe photographs or videos being taken or shown, interviewers should also inquire into this aspect of abuse. Even if the child describes only innocuous photos, interviewers should always consider the possibility that the offender has not yet reached the point with this child of more explicit imagery or that the child is so embarrassed by the existence of the photographs that she will not disclose their nature or confirm they were ever taken. Even when presented with the actual photographs or tapes, some children will continue to deny their own identity. This is especially true if the victim is a preadolescent or adolescent male.

During the disclosure process the interviewer needs to maintain a neutral expression, no matter what the child is saying. In many instances, the child will not initially reveal all of the incident or incidents. MacFarlane (1985) has described the disclosure process as "peeling the onion," with the child describing the least traumatic event first and gradually giving up the more disturbing information as she assesses the reaction of the people with whom she is talking. It is not uncommon to need more than one interview to get the necessary information (Sorensen & Snow, 1991).

The disclosure process is like "peeling the onion."

If the interviewers have still photographs of this child that are believed to have been taken by the offender, then a protocol needs to be established on how to present these to the child, if it is necessary to the case. How this is done can be critical. No photograph should be given greater weight than any other in this process. We suggest that a photograph notebook be compiled with all photos included *before* the interview. Place one photograph per page with a number or letter below it. A blank sheet should be placed between each photo page. The least sexually explicit photos should be at the front of the book, followed by the more graphic ones.

After the issue of photos has been brought up, the child will be asked to look through the book and answer at least three questions about each picture: Who took it? Where was it taken? What is happening in the picture? Investigators should never spring pictures on a child without warning, and they should not set the child up by asking if pictures were taken when they know they were and have them in their possession. The child should simply be told that the team has photographs of her and that it would like her to look at them. If some of the photographs are sexually explicit, then neither cover up any part of the photo nor indicate disgust or other emotions by expression or affect that may be interpreted negatively by the child. When finished going through the notebook with the child, the investigator should put it out of the child's sight for the remainder of the interview. After the interview has been completed, the notebook should be put in the child's file intact, with none of the photos removed for use in other interviews. The notebook thus becomes an extremely important piece of evidence.

As another person views or listens to any audio- or videotape made of the interview, he or she has the notebook as a ready reference as to what the child is describing. Should more than one child appear in the photographs, make extra sets of prints so that each child's file will have its own photographic notebook.

One area that needs to be thoroughly covered in an intrafamilial situation is the extent to which a nonoffending parent or caretaker was or is aware of the abuse. Questions should be asked to determine how the child gets along with her parent(s); how the parent(s) punish the child; whether the parent(s) know about the sexual abuse; whether the child has told the parent(s) about the abuse and, if so, how long ago; what exactly the child has told the parent(s); what the parent(s) did about it; whether the child thinks the parent(s) will believe her; whether the parent(s) will help the child; whether the child believes the parent(s) will act in a manner to protect the child from the offender; how the parent(s) get along with the offender and other family members; and what the best and worst things are about her parent(s). The interviewers can also observe if the child is protective of the nonoffending parent (possible role reversal). Is the child talking spontaneously, or is she concealing information or acting fearful? How anxious is the child to be with her parent? Is the child saying she cannot go home and must have somewhere else to stay?

It would be unrealistic to believe that every child interviewed will be forthcoming with statements of abuse, even when abuse has taken place. Remember that there are many instances when abuse has not occurred and that the interviewer must determine nonabuse cases as well as abuse cases. Professionals working in the child abuse field in the past few years have been accused of going on witch-hunts and finding abuse under every rock. Interviewers who can maintain their objectivity and look critically at both the verbal and nonverbal information given by children during the interviews are going to be better able to refute possible charges of overzealousness in the legal forum, where many of these cases end up.

Realistically, not all children in all interviews will be totally truthful in all of their statements. Some seemingly apparent "lies" on the part of the child may have been caused by the interviewer asking confusing questions or misunderstanding the child's response.

How to handle a child who is not being truthful during the interview is a delicate matter. For many children, a light approach works as well as a direct confrontation. For example:

Child: I have a phone in my room.
Lead: You do? And you're only 6 years old! What is your phone number?
Child: (Pause) 5-5-5-2-4. . . .
Lead: Are there any more numbers?
Child: Nope. That's it.
Lead: Well, I think it has more numbers. Maybe when I talk to your mom she can tell me what the whole number is. That way I can call you.
Child: (Pause) Well, I don't exactly have a phone in my room, (rushed) but I'm going to get one soon.
Lead: Okay, I'm glad you cleared that up for me. Remember that when we are talking today, we only talk about things that are real. Can you try hard to do that?

For the older child whom the interviewer believes is possibly fabricating (either by omission or commission), it might well be possible to take a more direct approach. One could point out that the information the child has shared does not fit known facts. In some ways the situation is analogous to that of interviewing a suspect. It may be necessary to discuss some of the potential reasons why a possible victim is denying abuse when there is firm evidence (e.g., photos of the abuse or the presence of a sexually transmitted disease). If the interviewer feels the abusive or exploitative situation described by the child is not accurate, then the interviewer needs to open the door and talk about the problems that he or she has with the statement. For example:

Lead: Mary, I want to get this straight. Correct me if I say something that is different from what you told me. David had you go down on him on the front porch and came, right?

Mary (16 years old): Right. I spit it out as soon as I could. It was really gross.

Lead: And about 10 minutes later you walked around the house and he pushed you up against the house and tried to put his penis in you.

Mary: Yeah.

Lead: He was fully erect or had a real hard-on, I think is what you said.

Mary: Yeah.

Lead: Well, Mary, I think we need to talk about this some more. I'm having a problem seeing how that could happen. David is 52 years old, and men of that age just don't usually get erections every 10 minutes.

The investigators will need to be alert throughout the interview to signals from the child that suggest the need to cease questioning and terminate the interview. Some interviewers tend to persist asking questions if the child continues to answer, even if she shows fatigue or anxiety. The interviewer should be considerate of the child's needs and take a break or even terminate the interview for the day, if feasible. As the child begins to tire, becomes thirsty, hungry, or needs to go to the bathroom, interviewers need to act as soon as it comes to their attention. If the child does not bring the need up, the interviewer can ask after awhile whether a break is needed. To continue questioning in the face of a tiring or fidgeting child has no benefits. The child may feel that the interviewers do not really care about her but only "like" her if she is answering questions. Continuing to say, "Just one more question" for 30 minutes and 15 more questions may destroy any trust and goodwill the interviewers have built.

A major factor to consider is how problematic it will be to schedule another interview. If there are legitimate concerns that parents may not cooperate or may actively work against the investigation, or the alleged offender will have access to the child, then it may pay to expand the interview time, providing frequent breaks. Of additional concern is that an adolescent female who fancies herself "in love" with the offender may contact him as soon as possible and warn him that an investigation is underway.

When the lead concludes his or her questioning and passes the session to the secondary interviewer who asks any additional or clarifying questions necessary, this interview should be brought to an end. If appropriate to the child's age, a last question can be posed: "If you were me, are there any questions I should ask that I didn't?" It is not uncommon for the child to give specific questions leading to detailed abuse-related information. As adults, we do not always know what questions will trigger a disclosure.

Termination of the interview should be accomplished with just as much tact as its beginning. The child should be informed that the interviewer has asked all of the questions that he or she needs to ask now, but that she may need to be interviewed again. The child should be thanked for her cooperation and patience. The interviewer should refer to the statement at the interview's beginning that she would be given a chance to ask questions and fulfill that promise. She may ask what will happen to the offender, her family, or herself. Responses should be truthful but general in nature: "To tell you the truth, I don't know what is going to happen to David [the offender]. My job is to ask questions and find out what happened and then tell other people who will make decisions about David. The important thing for you to remember is that what happens to David is not because of you, but because of what he did. Grown-ups are supposed to know what they can do with kids, and it's up to them to do right." Some children will need additional reassurance that they are not in trouble.

When the child has no more questions, a brief explanation as to what will happen next is in order. This might include a medical examination or interviews with other family members. The child might express some concern over telling her parents what she has shared in the interview. The interviewer can tell the child that he or she cannot keep all that the child has said private because other people have to know in order to help make sure it does not happen again. Whatever the interviewer does, he or she should not lie to the child or make promises that will be impossible to keep. Information shared cannot be kept secret, an absolute promise that abuse will never happen again is unrealistic (we wish it were not), and life, as the child knows it, may drastically change as a result of the investigation.

For the child who has not disclosed abuse, termination of the interview is different in some respects. Again, the child is thanked for her patience and answering questions as best she could. If the interviewer feels that the child was not abused and that no other interviews or investigative action will take place, then it may be appropriate to tell the child that this is the end of the matter and that the interview took place because someone was concerned about the child. The child should be afforded the opportunity to ask questions. If the child is old enough, the interviewer can provide a business card for the child to save and use should she feel a need to talk to the investigator in the future.

If the child has not disclosed, but investigators feel or have independent evidence that abuse has occurred, then the team must decide how best to proceed. It is generally best to let the child know that the interviewers are concerned about her and that they feel they need to talk to more people. The child can be told that the interviewers will probably be talking to the child again. For example:

Lead: You know, when I ask questions of boys and girls like I asked you today, they sometimes have trouble remembering. Then later, they think of stuff they think I might want to know. That's okay. Even grown-ups do that. If that happens, I want you to know that you can call me or your mother can call me and we'll come and talk to you again. It won't make us mad or anything.

You can call even if you don't think it's very important. Just let us know. Okay?

Or:

Lead: Part of our job is to talk to everybody who might know something we need to know. After we do this, we'll probably come back to talk to you. You may think of some stuff later that can help us, and we want to give you a chance to tell us.

For adolescents, the interviewer might choose to be even more direct, stating that the interviewer thinks (feels, knows) that there is more to the situation than the child has disclosed. The investigator may want to tell the child that the investigation is not going to stop just because she was not ready to talk about the situation. This can be a frustrating position when investigators have a child who would be an excellent witness because of age, maturity, observational ability, and ability to express herself. It does no good to get angry. Provide the child with a means of getting in touch with one of the investigators and emphasize an interest in talking at any time the child wants.

When the team believes abuse has occurred but a younger child has not disclosed, the team may decide to refer the child for extended assessment, which is conducted by a mental health professional working with the team.

When the interview is concluded, the investigative team should meet to review any information obtained and, based on this information, make decisions on how best to proceed.

7

Corroborating Interviews

After interviewing the alleged victim, investigators should also talk with any other children identified as possible victims or witnesses for information about their possible abuse or to gather any corroborating or conflicting information. The child witnesses may not have direct knowledge of the sexual abuse, but they may be able to confirm important aspects of the alleged victim's statement. For example, another child may be able to confirm that the victim told him or her of overtures or sexual activity on the part of the offender long before disclosures were made to adults, or he or she may be able to confirm elements of the victim's statement; the witness may have seen the perpetrator leave the victim's room or heard the victim's cries, or the child may simply describe the household routine that allowed the offender to be alone with the victim, as has been alleged.

> *Child witnesses may be able to confirm the alleged victim's statement.*

Always consider the possibility that all of the children living in the household with an offender or with whom he has private contact might have been victimized. Even offenders who appear to have gender preferences have been known to engage in abusive behavior with children of the other gender. If their interview with the index child (the child originally identified) leads investigators to the conclusion that other children may have been victimized, they need to act swiftly to secure interviews with these children. The same safeguards and questioning protocols that were used with the first child victim should be used with any other child interviewed. Should the investigation indicate a preferential child molester (an individual who prefers to engage in sexual activity with children rather than with individuals in his own age group), then any child who has come into private contact with the individual should be considered a possible victim or witness and interviewed. (See also Chapter 11's discussion of macro case investigations.)

❏ Nonoffending Parent Interview

In intrafamilial cases, the so-called nonoffending parent, who is most commonly the mother (and the gender used in this chapter), will be the next family member interviewed in-depth. Frequently, this is the most difficult interview for the investigator. Historically, the professional literature has often held the mother responsible for the abuse, at least in part, in incest cases (Salter, 1988), and even today a minority of professionals attribute significant blame to the mother for intrafamilial sexual abuse (Ards & Harrell, 1993). Any natural bias of the interviewer may be further influenced if the child has stated that this parent knew of the abuse through direct observation or from the child. Although interviewers may feel less than neutral when talking to this party, a nonjudgmental attitude must be maintained to gain accurate information.

From the social service perspective, this important assessment must be made to determine whether the child can remain with the mother during the rest of the investigation. The investigative interview focus for law enforcement personnel is (a) to learn what the nonoffending parent believes happened and what she has been told, (b) to find corroborative evidence to support or refute the child's statement or the statement of the alleged offender, and (c) to work with the social worker to assess the parent's ability and willingness to protect the child so that she will have a supportive environment. This environment is necessary for the child to begin the healing process and enhance her ability to handle the challenges that the legal system demands of the sexual abuse survivor.

This interview, like that of the child, should be conducted in a neutral setting if at all possible. (If team members decide that a crime scene search of the child's home for evidence of the abuse is necessary, then they may want to interview the nonoffending parent at the home and attempt to obtain a consent to search from her at the time of this interview.) Only the interviewers and the parent should be present. Because of the nature of some of the questions that the interviewer may ask the parent (such as spousal violence or quality, quantity, and type of sexual activity engaged in with the offending parent), privacy should be maintained.

During the early stages of the interview, investigators should convey an attitude of concern for the child and the nonoffending parent. Neither guilt nor recriminations should be put forth by interviewers, who should reassure the parent as much as possible that there is a legitimate reason, not only for this interview but also for certain questions that will be asked. The interviewer's attitude should be that of a seeker of truth trying to discover what actually happened, not someone out to convict any individual or imply that this person is a poor or neglecting parent.

In general, investigators want to determine what the parent knows about the sexual abuse. Interviewers should tell the parent only as much as absolutely necessary about the child's disclosure and not reveal anything during this interview that they do not wish to have repeated to the perpetrator. It is frequently best to use generalities, at least in the early stages of the interview.

Even if this parent reported the allegation, there will be several possible reactions to this information, ranging from anger and grief to disbelief and hostility. The interviewer might find it necessary to give the parent several minutes to ventilate and express her feelings before bringing the interview back on track (Sgroi, 1982). When the parent expresses anger, it may be general in nature and yet directed at the child, investigators, what the child has told, or the perpetrator. Some of this anger, particularly that directed at the interviewers, is an attempt to gain and maintain control of the situation. Usually, when we first talk with the nonoffending parent, she is in shock. Many times she does not know or has denied to herself that the abuse has been taking place. Sometimes she has known something was not right or seemed unusual, but she has not suspected child abuse. In some cases, she knew something was going on but feared that she was crazy or reading things into an innocent situation. This may well be the case if she is a survivor of child sexual abuse herself. At other times, she may actually have known the abuse was going on, or the child told her about the abuse and either she did not believe it or became angry and told the child not to talk about it. Perhaps she confronted the perpetrator and he denied it or promised that it would never happen again. This response is the most difficult for us to accept and handle. The way to understand it is to begin to understand why it is happening.

> When a mother suspects or is told of incest, she faces simultaneous and overlapping tasks: (1) assessing the accuracy of the information, (2) determining the meaning of incest to her and her family, (3) deciding what to do with the new information, and (4) locating and using resources. Revelation of intrafamilial sexual abuse can occur in one of several ways, each of which poses its own set of challenges. However, the tasks remain essentially the same. . . . [M]others who are told of the incest by the child, another family member, or someone outside the family may either acknowledge or deny the reality of the information confronting them. However, the context of such a reevaluation makes it more difficult to discount the information, particularly if the incest is revealed to the mother by protective services or law enforcement personnel. Mothers who observe clues of possible sexual abuse have had more opportunity to integrate the information before the abuse is confirmed. . . . Mothers who are told without having observed any signs of abuse have no shield against the shock of such devastating news. . . . Given the opportunity, mothers of incest victims will articulate the confusion typical of a crisis state. (Elbow & Mayfield, 1991, p. 76)

Believing that her husband or boyfriend has abused her child forces a woman to make choices and take actions. If she has already decided to end the relationship or is on the brink of this decision, then she is more likely to believe the child. The woman who wants to remain in the relationship or who at least has mixed feelings has the hardest time. She is angry at her child for not telling sooner or stopping the abuse. She is angry at the perpetrator for doing this to her child or her. She feels guilty. She has failed to protect her child, and she has failed to satisfy her husband or lover. She thinks it may be her fault that this has happened. She feels betrayed by her husband or boyfriend because he has been living a lie; she feels betrayed by her child for having kept the relationship a secret. She hates her partner for the consequences of what he has done and the damage to the child, her relationship with her own child, and the relationship between the two of them. He has caused all the trauma everyone is now experiencing. She is repulsed by thoughts of him touching her child and is trying to get these thoughts out of her mind. She also may feel jealousy toward her daughter or son for the extra attention and what she perceives to be the special relationship that the child seems to have with the offender.

Mostly, she is confused. On the one hand she wants to support and help her child, but one does not simply change one's feelings for someone even when learning about sexual abuse. There are new feelings that compete with the old ones. She feels caught between the two, not sure what is best. Most of all she feels that she not only has failed as wife and mother but also is now expected to take charge of resolving all of the problems that resulted, even though she was not directly involved with the abuse and may not have known about it.

Women in this position often are the ones who are less able to cope with making these choices. It is important that we take their background into consideration: Have they been abused sexually or physically? What are their dependency issues? Is the dependency financial, emotional, or both? If she is faced with the possible loss of a breadwinner or, at the very least, a drastically decreased standard of living, not to mention any love or attachment she might feel, what will she do? She may be afraid of being alone or feel that she owes it to the relationship to stay. She is going backward and forward in her feelings.

If her husband or boyfriend is adamantly denying that the abuse occurred or is minimizing or blaming the child or the mother for what happened, then it is much harder on the mother. To stand up for her child, she must stand up to him.

The nonoffending parent needs all the support she can get during the crisis.

In many of these relationships there has been physical or verbal intimidation or unequal power balance. This is the hardest crisis that a woman may ever have to face. What she does will have long-term consequences for herself, her children, and her family. She needs all the support she can get (Herring, 1991).

Sometimes a nonoffending parent will be quite concerned about what will happen to her rather than show concern about the child's immediate well-being. The interviewer can make it clear to her that these issues will be discussed at a later time.

It is necessary for the investigator(s) to determine how much of the child's statement the parent can corroborate or refute. As in all interviews, it is frequently best to let the parent talk about her knowledge in a flowing narrative style and then return and ask specific questions at the end of the parent's narrative.

❑ Specifics to Be Covered

The following specifics should be addressed:

1. Can the parent confirm any behavioral indicators?
2. Does the parent recall any times when the opportunity existed for the alleged abuse to take place? What are the times when her partner had private access to the child or children?
3. How long has the nonoffending parent known or suspected the abuse or allegation of abuse?
4. How did the parent become aware of the alleged abuse or allegation?
5. Does the parent believe that the child is telling the truth or that the abuse is possible?
6. Now that the child has disclosed, and looking back, were there any unusual incidents (things the child or alleged offender said, physical injuries, behavioral changes, strange occurrences, etc.) that might shed light on the allegations?

7. Can she empathize with the child's current emotional state after the disclosure?

8. What is the child normally like?

9. What is her relationship like with the child? How do they solve problems? Do they use punishment?

10. Where does she want the child to be pending completion of the investigation?

11. Will she cooperate in having the alleged offender leave the home and have no contact between the child and the alleged offender so that the child can remain at home?

12. Will she agree to seek medical and counseling services for the child and herself?

13. What information can she provide about the alleged offender?

Does he use alcohol or other drugs? How much? How often? With whom? Where?

Has he shown a loss of control over other behaviors (i.e., smoking, gambling, battering)?

What are his sleep habits? Is he the last to bed, up at night, or the first to rise?

Has he initiated prolonged physical contact with the child (i.e., tickling without stopping)?

Does he look at pornography? What kinds? How much? How often? Does he want her to engage in it?

Does he have difficulty accounting for his time? Is his time unstructured? Does he cruise in the car with no destination? Does he have unexplained mileage?

How does he exhibit discipline? Does he show favoritism? Is he harsh or erratic? Does he bestow gifts? Does he have pet names for the children? What are they?

Does he wear inappropriate apparel (e.g., robe only, no underwear, broken zipper)?

Does he leave the bedroom or bathroom door ajar when he is engaged in activities that should be private?

Does he have unusual job stress? Has he been fired, laid off, or endured a change in job description?

Has he undergone a rapid religious conversion?

Has he been involved in youth programs? Has he shown an unusually high interest in neighborhood kids?

Does he isolate the child? Has he expressed negative interest in victim's social or sexual behavior (e.g., shown jealousy or complained about dates)?

Has he been unable to account for money, gifts, or loans?

Has there been a shift in parental responsibility?

Has he retreated to childhood as evidenced by clothing, language, or the cultivation of younger friends?

Have there been unresolved marital conflicts? Has he refused to discuss problems?

How does he spend time with the children?

What is his attitude toward sex offenders?

14. Who bathes and dresses the children?

15. What are the family's sleeping arrangements? What are the access opportunities?

16. How will she support herself and the child(ren) if her partner leaves the home? Where can he stay?

17. What will she do if he wants to come back?

18. What information can she provide about the child victim?

Does she have any sleep disturbances such as nightmares or bedwetting? What clothing does she sleep in?

Does she appear depressed at times? Does the child ever seem withdrawn or distant? Has the child talked of or joked about suicide or made any suicide plans or attempts?

Has she shown any changes in hygiene, appetite, or weight?

Does she try to avoid the offender? Has there been any change in how the victim refers to the alleged offender (e.g., from "Daddy" to first-name basis)?

Has the victim asked about parental marital or divorce status?

Has the child shown any unusual fears or anxieties? Does the child seem to cling to the nonoffending parent? Is the child unusually concerned about privacy?

Has there been any change in peer relationships? Is the child protective of younger siblings?

Have there been any legal problems such as theft or alcohol or drug use?

Has the child become physically or sexually aggressive toward or with others?

Has the child run away in the past? Has the child ever been pregnant or married early? Is he or she sleeping elsewhere? Does the child come home late?

Have there been any physical indicators such as infections, rashes, abrasions, or bleeding?

> With the young child, have there been any mysterious codes or nonsense secrets with the alleged offender? Do they seem to have serious overtones?

(These items were adapted from material from the Rape and Sexual Abuse Center's *Partner Alert List*, by O. Ring and Northwest Treatment Associates.)

A mother who has acted appropriately by reporting suspected or known abuse is likely to be viewed favorably by the investigators, but the reality is that some observers in court and elsewhere will question *why* she reported the abuse. There is a tendency to reformulate mothers' reporting as vindictive rather than protective. Some have suggested that a mother who reports sexual abuse may falsely accuse a divorcing husband in an effort to support a case for custody (Elbow & Mayfield, 1991).

Like the child interview, the adult interview will move from the general, less threatening areas to more sensitive issues. Once the interviewer has an idea of family dynamics, he or she can move to more delicate areas. It is difficult to begin the conversation asking about family members' arrest histories or psychiatric treatment. It would seem normal to inquire about marital history early in the process. The interviewers are seeking to establish an alliance with the nonoffending parent. They might well want to obtain permission to search the premises for evidence that would support or refute the child's statement. Even the ability to observe the home as the child described it can aid investigators in their determination of the accuracy of the information provided by the child. This may be an opportune time for the officer to ask the mother for a signed consent to search the premises and remove any physical evidence.

In introducing the issue of sexual abuse, the interviewers may find it necessary to share with the parent short but dramatic portions of the child interview tape or other products of the interview such as drawings or letters to the offender. During the entire process, interviewers assess her reactions, responses, and reality. How does the nonoffending parent react to the team and to the prospect of further involvement with CPS and law enforcement? If the parent is appropriately concerned, believes the child, and supports the goals of the investigation, then she can be enlisted as an ally of the team in helping the child.

If this parent's attitude toward the victim is unbelieving or unsupportive, hostile, punitive, or rejecting, then she cannot be considered properly protective of the victim. Out-of-home placement of the child should be considered with CPS.

The interviewers should be aware of the services that are available for spouses and children such as temporary shelters, financial assistance, and medical and psychological assistance. It is preferable to have this information in a written form that can be left with a parent. This will be useful later when she will need to have a concrete way to recall the information.

If possible, the interview should end on a positive note, with the nonoffending parent given a card with the interviewer's name and telephone number and the direction to call if she needs any help or thinks of anything that would help the child. It is important to give the parent a contact for a support group or other mechanism to assist her through the initial stages of the investigative process. One of her needs is to have someone to talk to and the knowledge that she is not the only one to have gone through this. Investigators should start to prepare the parent for the intervention of the criminal justice system such as the possibility of preliminary hearings, grand jury proceedings, and medical examinations. Interviewers can attempt to address concerns and answer questions that the parent has at this time.

For law enforcement professionals, the exploration of possible charges against a nonoffending parent who failed to protect the child, report the abuse, or even helped set up the abuse should be considered with the prosecutor. Document any evidence that supports charges of complicity in the sexual abuse of or failure to protect the child.

❏ Parents in Out-of-Home Abuse Cases

The interview with parents in extrafamilial cases is generally appropriate after the child has been interviewed (in some cases, it will be more appropriate to interview these parents first when their knowledge of the child's contacts with the offender or personal habits will assist in preparing for the child interview). The interviewers are interested in what the child has told the parents about the assault(s) and in physical or behavioral indicators that the parents may have observed. In cases in which the offender is known by the family, investigators want to explore the parent's relationship with the offender, how they first met the offender, what the offender told them he or she was doing with their child, and how he or she responded to any particular questions they might have had about activities with the child. Any material the offender may have given the child such as gifts, letters, and photographs should be secured or otherwise documented.

Investigators must determine whether parents believe the child and what plan they can develop to reduce the risk of further abuse. An explanation of what steps must be taken as part of the investigative process, as well as the possibility that the child may recant the disclosure, should be given. Parents can be given instructions on how to handle additional disclosures by the child and information on whom to contact if they have problems or questions or need additional information.

Attitudes of parents in these cases varies. Some parents may be supportive of their children and the goals of the investigation; others may be more concerned with issues that are not paramount to investigators. Considerable extrafamilial abuse occurs when the child is breaking a family rule, either on her own or with the encouragement of the offender. To disclose the sexual abuse to the parent means also to disclose her own disobedience. Some of the infractions may seem trivial to an uninterested bystander, yet to the child smoking a cigarette, taking a swig of beer, or looking at a sexually explicit periodical may seem deserving of profound punishment. All too often interviewers find when dealing with the family that the first parental response is anger at the child for doing something she knew should not be done; the issue of sexual abuse seems secondary. Children may not know how their parents will react to the disclosure of abuse, but they usually have a long, accurate history of the parental reaction to rule breaking. The interviewers have to deal with this in their interview with the child and be prepared to handle it in the interview with the parents.

As with the nonoffending spouse, the investigators should be prepared to discuss with the parents the normal steps in the investigation and how they can best assist their child in going through the process. The whole family will be affected by this situation, and it is not uncommon for the entire family to need some sort of counseling. The team is in the best position to know what is available for the child and family and should present that information to them in written form.

An issue that frequently arises in out-of-home abuse situations has to do with media attention. When a troop leader, choir master, or teacher is alleged to be the abuser, media interest will be high. Informing the parents of this before media representatives descend will be of help to the family. Informing the family of its rights and the rights of the child may help them in making decisions about how to deal with this phenomenon. Being clear as to who team members are and what sort of identification the parents need to see before allowing anyone they do not know can prevent unscrupulous private investigators or reporters who may attempt to talk with the child. The parents should be thoroughly directed to contact the investigators they have met if they have concerns or questions. Business cards should be provided for this purpose.

Inform parents that media interest will be high.

❏ Other Credible Adult Interviews

During the investigative process, investigators will be interviewing other professionals who may have information or knowledge that may be of use to the team. This could include a history of relevant physical or emotional problems and changes in behavior patterns, as well as relevant statements made by any of the principals. These professionals might include teachers, physicians, nurse practitioners, mental health professionals, and those identified as experts in various aspects of child abuse. In most of these interviews, neither the individual nor the information he or she provides will be perceived as unusually tainted or prejudiced. The same cannot be said of interviews with some other adults. Relatives, neighbors, church contacts, and others might provide critical information, but their objectivity must be carefully assessed.

The issue of motivation and credibility of those who provide information in criminal cases has always been critical in the legal system. From the narcotics informant who is paid for the deal he arranges to the eyewitness who provides the identification of a robber, certain individuals will always challenge the thought processes that lead the person who assists in an investigation. Child sexual abuse cases are no exception. As they listen to statements of adults, investigators should mentally assess witnesses' motivation, credibility, and objectivity. This is true whether the statement supports or contradicts the child's statement. Discounting information that contradicts a child's statement during the investigation may result in an unpleasant surprise in court. To accept without question any information that supports the child may mean that a key witness on the stand can be discredited by a defense attorney, an event that could have been avoided or planned for if healthy skepticism had been present during the initial interview.

Credibility depends not only on the individual but also on the circumstances. A grandmother whose granddaughter has been sexually abused by a teacher may be able to provide perfectly accurate information about behavioral indicators or specific details the girl shared with her about the relationship with the offender. However, if the offender was alleged to be her beloved son or despised former son-in-law, then her information must be viewed differently—again, perhaps as completely accurate, but also perhaps as biased in one way or another.

Collateral interviews are extremely important in helping the team compile a balanced picture of the overall situation. These should always be attempted, even when investigators feel that they have clear and convincing evidence of the proof of the allegations or the guilt of the accused. Sometimes funny things happen on the way to the courtroom, and the investigators should be aware of all the pitfalls along the way.

8

Other Investigative Considerations

In many instances the investigator is limited only by the scope of his or her imagination and legal parameters. Keeping an open mind to new investigative techniques or those not typically used in child sexual abuse cases can lead investigators to previously unattainable solutions. These strategies and techniques are drawn from broader law enforcement knowledge and experience and include proper crime scene work, DNA analysis, recorded pretext conversations, and lineups.

❑ Crime Scene

The use of the crime scene search is often overlooked in child abuse cases, particularly intrafamilial cases. As in other types of crimes, this can be an extremely helpful technique. Not only can a crime scene search uncover evidence of crime, but it can also support aspects of the child's statement and thus lend greater credibility to his or her information.

Preparation for a search and conducting the actual search is the responsibility of the team's law enforcement members. Although other team members may have information to contribute such as details about items they might have seen in the home while there, they have no legal authority to seize items for evidentiary purposes. Law enforcement officials may not use social counselors to circumvent legal protections against unreasonable searches. Any evidence obtained in such a manner will be excluded in court, should the case go there.

In an intrafamilial case in which the nonoffending spouse has equal access to the area to be searched, he or she can be asked to sign a search consent. The officers need to be aware of their legal limitations if they come to an area that is off-limits to the spouse or find locked containers or areas for which the spouse has no keys. At that point, it would be wise to consult with the prosecutor.

In other circumstances a search warrant should be obtained. Many children, if questioned about physical evidence, will be able to tell interviewers what it looks like and where it is stored. If a child has confirmed that the offender took photographs, then interviewers should ask other questions about the type of camera (e.g., video, 35-mm, Polaroid), where the offender got the camera, what he did with the pictures or tape, where he put them afterward, and any other pieces of information that could be used to support a search warrant.

Most state laws specify what is necessary to obtain a warrant (see Box 8.1). A search warrant can be issued only on probable cause; it must be supported by affidavit, and it must name or describe the person, and especially the property and the place to be searched. "Probable cause" is a reasonable ground of suspicion, supported by circumstances sufficiently strong in themselves to warrant a cautious person in the belief that the accused is guilty of the offense charged.

The officer must list the items for which he or she is looking. There are five general categories of evidence being sought:

1. fruits of the crime,
2. instrumentalities used to commit the crime,
3. weapons or like materials that might present a danger to the officer,

---

Box 8.1: Search Warrant Requirements

The following requirements must be met for a search warrant
to be issued:

1. Probable cause must be shown.
2. The warrant must be supported by an affidavit.
3. It must name or describe the person sought.
4. It must describe the property and place to be searched.
5. It must state specifically what is being sought.

---

4. contraband, and
5. anything that constitutes evidence of the crime and connects the
   suspect to it.

The affidavit, which is an attachment to the warrant, needs to spell
out the affiant's training and experience that enables him or her to
recognize the significance of items that might be found at the scene
of the search but which are not enumerated in the warrant. The
warrant needs to be drafted as broadly as possible to allow the
searchers to seize everything they find that is pertinent to the case,
the motivation of the offender, the level of interest in children, and
the identities of other unknown victims.

Crime scene preservation needs to be practiced as much as prac-
ticable. The purpose of crime scene preservation is twofold: (a) to
effect a complete reconstruction of events with respect to the se-
quence of events, method of operation, motive, and whatever else
the criminal may have done; and (b) to recover the clues that will
serve as evidence against the criminal.

The general crime scene search procedure includes several preliminary steps: identification of the person who first notified the
authorities; determination of the perpetrator by direct inquiry or
observation; detention or identification of all people at the scene; the
safeguarding and physical isolation of the area; separation of witnesses; and protection of the evidence from handling or removal. A
plan of search that will cover all the ground and evidence should be
seen as establishing one or more of the following: the *corpus delicti,*

or the fact that the crime was committed; the perpetrator's method of operation; and the identity of the guilty person.

The law enforcement investigator should be prepared to deal with any search from a school building or church to a small trailer or park playground. The search team can react swiftly in securing possible evidence if it has readily available a camera (video or 35-mm), tape recorder and tape, notebook, labels, paper bags, cardboard boxes, and protective gloves.

The officer must remember that identifying evidence and preserving the scene is not enough; the evidence must be correctly tagged, packaged, and attributed and then submitted to the laboratory in a timely manner if lab tests are needed. The chain of custody must be maintained, and appropriate storage must be provided. Those officers who work in departments that can afford such high-tech items should bring their laptop or notebook comput-

Evidence must be correctly tagged, packaged, and attributed.

ers to the scene; crime scene software is available that allows the logical cataloging of evidence. An appropriate printer will also be able to make evidence labels and give the officer an accurate and fast printout for interested parties.

Specific items that the investigators want to look for include but are not limited to the following: child-oriented books, magazines, and articles; video equipment and cameras; photos, negatives, slides, movies, videocassettes, and drawings of children; personal letters and other correspondence from others who are sexually interested in children; diaries; sexual aids; "souvenirs" of the sexual interaction; toys, games, or other lures or enticements used by the offender to gain or maintain the interest of children; personal computers and software; weapons; bed clothes or other fabric that might contain evidence of body fluids or pubic hair; and lists of other victims or offenders (Lanning, 1982).

When collaborating with federal authorities, additional seizures, such as automobiles and other real property, may be made. Police agencies should discuss with their attorneys petitioning the court for ownership of items used by the offender that have been legally seized and which are potentially useful to the department. These might include computers, televisions, video equipment, cameras, and VCRs.

Even if the child has detailed no specific items that might be seized, it is to the investigator's advantage to memorialize the scene described by the child as soon after the interview as possible. This can be done by still or video camera. The greater the delay, the greater the likelihood that the suspect or others will destroy or alter the scene in an effort to diminish the credibility of the child as an accurate historian or to cover up indicators of abuse that the child may not have shared. Waiting weeks or months before acting can be fatal to a case.

❑ DNA Analysis

Many years ago, scientists discovered the material in human genes, *deoxyribonucleic acid* (DNA), that carries genetic information and determines individual characteristics. In the early 1980s, it was first used in a criminal investigation. Many parts of DNA are the same from person to person, but other parts are nonfunctioning sequences that greatly vary. The variability can be studied and traced to an individual. In cases in which investigators have removed blood, semen, saliva, or tissue samples from a victim, technicians can submit them to laboratory examination. Blood specimens from the victim and alleged offender can be compared and the origin of a forensic specimen can often be determined. The possibility of misidentification is remote.

DNA testing requires a small amount of material: Bloodstains the size of a dime or semen samples the size of a quarter may suffice (C. Howard, personal communication, 1992). On semen samples, if the suspect has had a vasectomy, the test results may be negative. Controlled blood samples should be taken in an EDTA (purple top) tube. Semen or bloodstains on fabric should be air dried before packaging for shipment. Specimens should be packaged for shipment with three barriers between the sample and the person handling the package (e.g., EDTA tube in a sealed plastic evidence bag in a mailing container). They can be sent by registered mail or hand carried. The FBI laboratory, some state laboratories, and several private labs can conduct DNA testing. The minimum turnaround time from any laboratory, based on the amount of time it takes to conduct the specific tests, is approximately four weeks, with the average being six to eight.

❑ Pretext Conversations

An underused investigative technique is that of making controlled contact with the offender by the victim or victim's relatives. In certain situations this may resolve doubts harbored by investigators on particular points of the investigation. As with any other approach, there are occasions when this technique is more appropriate than others. It is not a panacea that will replace proper investigative techniques.

There are decisions and safeguards that the team must consider before it uses this technique. First and foremost, it should ask, "Is the contact necessary for the case?" If the same information and investigative goals can be reached through another means, that option should be used first. The team must consider the effect such contact would have on the victim or victim's family. It is wise to consult with both the prosecutor and the team's mental health consultant before raising this possibility with the family. Certain states' laws may make one-party consent recordings inadmissible in court, and this may make the procedure less desirable to a prosecutor. The mental health professional may feel that the child would be more traumatized by further contact, or he or she will help in structuring safeguards for the child or assist the child in processing emotions after contact has been made.

The child's age and her ability to carry on a conversation to elicit incriminating statements from the offender are of prime consideration. Getting the child's consent, as well as that of parents or guardian, is also important. In some jurisdictions it also may be necessary to obtain a court order to allow the child to assist in this process. Some children view this as an opportunity to assist with the investigation and see it as empowering.

> *Some children see these conversations as empowering.*

This may be important for the healing process. Investigators should frame the idea of contact with the offender as a request, taking care not to pressure the child or family. "This is the only way we'll ever know that you are not lying" and similar statements are inappropriate and counterproductive to the trust the team seeks to instill in the child.

The child and parents should know what the investigators' expectations are before they make their decisions. It is impossible to attempt to script a conversation for the child to follow. Even when working with adult survivors or adult relatives of the victim, it is extremely difficult to structure their portion of the call. Attempting to prepare for every contingency is not possible. It is more feasible to talk about areas in which there are specific legal needs (e.g., getting the offender to admit he engaged in the penetrating offense when the child was under 13 years of age). Giving the child permission to ask the offender questions over which she has stewed also may empower her. These questions most frequently revolve around why the abuse happened and why the offender chose this particular child.

The timing of the call is critical. If it is not done before the offender is aware of the investigation, the most likely outcome is a recording of a person voicing strong denials. This will be evidence and cannot be destroyed, and the tape will be available to defense attorneys later. Before the call is placed, all equipment should be checked to ensure that it works properly. If necessary, allow the child time to use and become more comfortable with it before calling the offender. In these days of call tracing or caller identification, make sure the call is made from a "safe" number. An undercover police line is probably the best, but the investigator must prepare for the question, "Where are you calling from?"

The child needs to be reassured that the call can be terminated at any time. It is possible that the mere sound of the offender's voice may render the child unable to continue with the call. The offender also may make statements that are calculated to manipulate the child or invoke emotions that are detrimental to the child's well-being. The team needs to prepare for this possibility and arrange a signal or mechanism by which it can terminate the call independently of the child. Support personnel must be immediately available for the child, if necessary.

The offender may not want to talk on the telephone and will request the child or cooperative caller to meet with him or her. The decision on how to handle this should be made before the call is placed. If the decision has been made by the victim and parents to allow a meeting, then the team needs to develop a strategy in which the child's safety is absolute and the investigators have control. Investigators will find this similar to setting up an undercover drug buy in which a significant amount of money must be protected. A face-to-face meeting necessitates the use of a body transmitter and a backup recorder of some type. Having a backup team in place to intervene if necessary is also mandatory.

This procedure should not be used with preadolescent children. There are simply too many physical and emotional dangers inherent in such a meeting. The best outcomes seem to be when the survivor is an older adolescent or adult. In fact, this technique has had extraordinary results in cases of adults reporting childhood sexual assault, even as far back as 50 years, where a state's statute of limitations allows such prosecution.

Should an incriminating recording be obtained, it can be most successfully used in confronting an offender. Reading a portion of the transcript or playing a compelling segment for the offender as he or she begins a denial can be a most useful technique for moving the interview to a constructive plane. Some recordings have been used in court and have been effective in combating defense attempts to portray the offender as an innocent party.

The primary caution to investigators is that the child is not responsible for the investigation or its success. This is an investigative technique to be used in selected circumstances with appropriate cooperating individuals and adequate safeguards in place. The child's welfare cannot be sacrificed to achieve the investigator's prosecutorial goals.

❑ Photo Lineups

Sometimes the child's identification of the offender will be imprecise in language, such as using a nickname like "Paw Paw" or a first name. Although investigators may believe that they know who the child means, it may be necessary to confirm the identity using either a photo or a live lineup. Children, however, do poorly on in-person lineups (Peters, 1991). The physical presence of the offender apparently increases stress and reduces the accuracy of the identification. Photo lineups reduce stress but raise other concerns that need to be addressed. Part of the problem is that some children do not understand the concept and have little understanding of what is expected of them. To combat the problem of acquainting children to adult expectations for photo lineups, the National Center for Missing and Exploited Children in 1986 recommended that officers conduct lineup work with children before actual suspect photos are shown. This preliminary exercise frames the experience for children. By clarifying what they are supposed to do, children are better able to respond accurately to interviewer questions about a perpetrator's identity.

Ideally, the person conducting this procedure is a team member with whom the child is familiar and has rapport. The focus of this conversation with the child is to ensure that he or she follows the interviewer's instructions exactly. The interviewer must do his or her best to discourage the child from providing responses merely to please the interviewer. A method for dealing with this is to teach the child the identification procedure. The first step involves showing the child several cards with objects on them and asking the child to select cards that match the interviewer's questions. For preschool children these might be five cards with a variety of simple shapes and colors. The child would then be asked to pick out the card with the red circle, blue square, and so on. Among the existing choices, the interviewer would also ask the child to select a color-and-shape combination that is not present. If the child is unclear on the concept, then she will typically select the closest card. For example, the child asked to pick out the purple square may well know that the square is blue but also the correct shape. Should this happen, the interviewer needs to tell the child to select only the exact item or combination asked for.

When the child has shown that she understands this level, the interviewer then moves on in complexity by presenting cards with more sophisticated images, such as animals or fruit. The same procedure is followed, with the child being asked to select the requested items. If the child, presented with a fruit series and told to pick out the apple (which is not present), selects the strawberry because it is the same color as an apple, the interviewer knows that the child is still operating on approximates. The interviewer must then again explain to the child that her job is to select only and exactly what is asked for. As the child demonstrates her understanding at this level, the investigator moves into people images.

The child is then presented with a series of photographs in the same format as the suspect photographs. This series of photos, however, is of individuals not suspected of abuse. For children molested by a male stranger, the photos might consist of women with the general description of the child's mother. The child is shown the lineup and asked to pick out a picture of her mother. The child who examines the grouping and then announces that her mother is not present shows an understanding of the procedure and the ability to comply with the investigator's request. This child is ready to proceed to the suspect lineup. The child who identifies one of the women as her mother should be questioned as to how she made the selection. If it was based on similarities between the actual mother and a photograph presented, the interviewer should discuss the differences with the child. It is necessary to determine if the child actually thought this woman was her mother. Inability to rule out erroneous selections should lead the interviewer to reconsider a photo lineup at this time. Consultation with a mental health professional as to why the child did not appear to understand the procedure might lead to additional avenues to pursue that would enable the child to deal successfully with the lineup procedure.

9

Interviewing the Suspect

The interview with the suspect is a situation that requires as much forethought as that of the interview with a child victim. There is no one best way to gain an admission or confession from sex offenders, because each individual will have differing motivations and gains from the behavior in which he or she has participated. The interviewer will have to look at the totality of information uncovered by the other interviews and the investigation as a whole in deciding what approach will be most successful in dealing with this individual.

Although we recognize that a growing number of females are identified as child sex offenders, this chapter will use masculine pronouns when referring to offenders.

❑ Preinterview Considerations

Many investigators, and some formal protocols, recommend that this important conversation be conducted at the conclusion of the evidence-gathering portion of the investigative process. This allows the interviewer to be fully cognizant of all of the information gathered and it has allowed time for a crime scene search or viewing, medical examination, and comprehensive background check of the accused. By having all of his or her "ducks in a row" before this interview, the interviewer is better prepared to detect false or misleading assertions on the part of the suspect and better prepared to counter defenses that may be erected to confuse the interviewer. For the suspect to be aware that the interviewer has visited the location where the abuse took place, has talked with the victim and other children, and has conducted a background check in places where the suspect formerly resided would seem to make it more difficult to be successfully deceptive. For the individual who has committed no crime, a thorough investigator can provide hope—hope that his name will be swiftly cleared because this detective is so thorough and prepared and has left no stone unturned, no question unasked.

The drawback to waiting until much of the investigation is completed before approaching the suspect is that it gives him time to prepare for the inevitable confrontation: preparation of alibis, possible intimidation of witnesses not yet interviewed, destruction of possible evidence, consultation with legal counsel who might advise noncooperation, fleeing the area, and, last but not least, committing an act of violence against himself or others. All are legitimate concerns for moving swiftly to confront this individual. The investigators need to make this decision on a case-by-case basis.

Much attention has been given in recent years to techniques for interviewing children, while relatively little has been focused on the adult offender interview. Surprisingly, many of the principles are similar, if not the same. Selection of the interview site can be critical. The principal psychological actor contributing to a successful interrogation is *privacy* (Inbau, Reid, & Buckley, 1986). Based on early assessment of the alleged offender, the investigator should decide whether it would be of greater benefit to conduct the interview in a place in which the offender would feel safer and more in control (thus divulging information that he might not if he felt really threatened) or whether it would help to put him off balance or keep him under pressure, such as could be provided during questioning in a law enforcement office. Consideration also must be given to the potential defendant's legal rights. Does Miranda apply in the situation being considered? Could the questioning be considered as or actually be a custodial interrogation? Does the team know whether he has legal representation? Is the offender a juvenile or mentally impaired, thus bringing into play different factors that will influence the courts' acceptance of any admission or confession? Recent legal decisions have affected our ability to conduct this important phase of the investigation, so the team must make decisions in this area in a planned, coordinated fashion.

This interview is seen as a primary function of the team's law enforcement member. Social service personnel may do the interview if the team decides that would be the most effective way to proceed. If the interview could be viewed as custodial in nature, then Miranda rights must be given regardless of what discipline the questioner comes from. If the decision is made by the team that it would be advantageous for a social service team member to conduct this interview, then the counselor must be aware of the legal ramifications of the way in which he or she questions the suspect. Such members also should remember to ask the factual who, what, when, why. and how questions that criminal investigators need for criminal prosecution.

> *This interview is a function of the team's law enforcement member.*

The interviewer's gender also may deserve consideration. Some offenders may have great difficulty in dealing with females in positions of power. They can be more reluctant to confide in a woman concerning their sexual activity or desires. It is also more difficult for females to use specific interview strategies that can be effective in dealing with male offenders. For example, note the following use of the "I understand" technique:

Male Interviewer: You know, I have a stepdaughter who is about Janie's age. A few weeks ago she got a new swimsuit, a bikini. I couldn't stop looking at her. She looked really sexy, really hot. I can understand how a normal guy could do something there. Is that how it happened, John?

Although this type of interviewing strategy has been perceived as useful only for male interviewers, a female interviewer can use a variation of this. In many instances, though, she will have a more difficult time convincing the suspect of her sincerity.

Female Interviewer: You know, I have a stepdaughter about Janie's age. I can't believe some of the clothes these girls wear. They prance around looking all hot to trot and then are so surprised when some guy buys what they are advertising. I mean some of these girls look like hookers. I can see how a normal guy might misunderstand the situation. Is that what happened here, John?

All interviewers need to be aware of any effect that their gender might be having on the interview. Although some men may not want to confess to a female, others may want to brag or attempt to shock the female interviewer. Inadvertently, he may give more information than intended and thus incriminate himself. Some men may view the female as such a little threat that they feel as if they can say anything without repercussions. During the course of the interview, should an interviewer of either gender (or any race or ethnic background, for that matter) see this as a stumbling block, then he or she should be professional enough to allow someone else of the other gender or different race or ethnic background who has prior knowledge of the case to pick up the questioning. There should not be any loss of face for turning over an unproductive interview to someone who may be better able to establish rapport or use an interviewing techniques that touches a chord with the suspect. It does not matter who asks the "magic question" or hits on the style that gets the confession; the important fact is that an admission or confession is obtained and that this may well make the process easier on the child or children.

A female suspect may well prefer to talk with another female. She may perceive the female interviewer to be a potential ally against the male system. It could well be that she has been abused in the past and would find it very difficult to talk to a male about these issues in any detail. If the suspect is part of a male and female abusing couple, then she may find it easier to talk about the dynamics of their situation (e.g., "He made me do it—it wasn't my idea") with another woman. We also have seen situations in which a female suspect's way of attempting to control the interview process will be through flirtation and by attempting to portray herself as a poor little woman who needs the understanding and protection of the big, strong male officer. All professionals should recognize these situations and use the range of interviewer and interview techniques to their advantage.

❏ The Interview

As mentioned earlier, privacy is a major factor in encouraging an individual to talk about this subject. If a person has a secret or problem, then he or she is not likely to confide this in front of several people (Inbau et al., 1986). The good interviewer will work to establish some level of rapport before launching into the discussion of sexual activities. The interviewer should be an impartial seeker of truth, an attitude that must be transmitted by any method possible to the suspect before the interview begins. This is much more effective than appearing to be so biased as to have little empathy for the alleged offender or a willingness to listen to what he has to say. If the interviewer

The interviewer should be an impartial seeker of truth.

gives the appearance of simply waiting for an excuse to throw the suspect into jail, then it is not likely that the suspect will want to aid the process. This requires that the interviewer control the normal indignation often felt after interviewing the victim.

Although selection of the interview site is critically important, the team needs to give some thought as to how the suspect is going to get there. Will he be interviewed in his home or workplace? How can the privacy that is so important be ensured? How will his feeling of safety provided by the familiar setting be overcome? How can interviewer safety be ensured? If investigators are going to have the suspect come to them, how will they get him there? Should he be picked up in a marked unit? How about an unmarked unit? Who will do the transporting? Do the transporting officers understand that they should keep their mouths shut and not offer opinions on what should happen to child abusers? An interviewer also can go to a lot of trouble to get a mental health opinion on the suspect and how to approach him and engage in rapport building. The interviewer can select the best interviewing site available and have the facts of the case down pat, but if other officers have had contact with the suspect and demean, threaten, or generally anger him before the interviewer meets him for the first time, the suspect may decline to participate. He also might have his guard so high that even the best interviewer will have a difficult time.

Will the suspect be called on the telephone and asked to come down to the station for a little chat? What will that do to the element of surprise that might otherwise be helpful? What is the next step if he declines? Is there enough evidence to pick him up and to ensure the victim's safety? The team has many basic decisions to make before seeing the alleged perpetrator.

We have no difficulty understanding the need to adopt the child's language and adjust questioning to the level of the child's understanding. The same, however, holds true for the offender. It is important to assess the suspect's level of comprehension and adjust the questioning to suit. As with children, many adults use terms they do not fully understand. When interviewers, in an attempt to be professional, use correct anatomical terms for body parts and clinical terms for sexual activity, the information obtained may be of questionable significance if it can be shown that the suspect did not understand the questions and blindly agreed with the interviewer on pertinent issues. For example:

Interviewer 1: Now, did you have an erection?
Suspect: A reaction?
Interviewer 1: An erection.
Interviewer 2: Use a word he understands.
Interviewer 1: Did you have a hard-on?
Suspect: Sort of. It was about halfway hard.
Interviewer 1: Did you ejaculate?
Suspect: Huh?
Interviewer 1: You know . . . did you come?
Suspect: Uh . . .
Interviewer 1: Did you get that certain feeling?
Suspect: Oh yeah! I got that feeling.

From the beginning of the interview, if the suspect will allow it, he should be treated with a measure of respect. If a confrontational atmosphere is established from the beginning, the investigator will not be able to backtrack later in the interview and become the "nice guy." The level of intensity can always be escalated; deescalation is extremely difficult. Some subjects respond well to this approach, saying that they did not realize that someone might understand them and the burden they had been carrying. As long as the suspect is cooperative, this stance can be maintained.

Even after the admission or confession has been obtained, the interviewer should not gloat; he or she should show compassion and provide the suspect with a means of contacting the investigator if the suspect thinks of anything else significant. Many of these men will later call with more details of the episode under investigation or give information on other, undiscovered victims. (Experience with female offenders has been limited, so we do not have a grasp of their general reaction to this approach.) This sometimes occurs even after attorneys have been consulted. The burden becomes lighter with each conversation. The interviewer should do whatever can be done to foster this process.

The interviewer should not make promises to the suspect that cannot be kept. It is tempting in the face of an offender who is clearly on the verge of confessing to promise diversion in lieu of incarceration or treatment programs rather than criminal prosecution. Such a promise not only will destroy any trust the suspect has developed with the interviewer but also risk making any subsequent confession inadmissible in court because of possible coercion.

According to Special Agent Kenneth Lanning of the FBI Academy's Behavior Sciences Unit, child sexual offenders have a fairly common pattern of response to questioning on child abuse issues (Lanning, 1992). The first response, unless caught in the act or presented with overwhelming evidence, is to deny completely any knowledge of any offense. The objective of the interviewer is to find a strategy to get the suspect past this denial (Lanning, 1992). Displaying belief in the abuse and emphasizing the need to be fair and get both sides of the story is one method of accomplishing this goal. A few offenders may attempt to maintain denial even after being caught in the act or being presented with photographs that clearly show them sexually engaged with a child.

Once an absolute denial has been abandoned, the investigator can move into more abuse-specific areas. It might take little effort to get the suspect to talk about his feelings for children or peripheral aspects of the abuse situation or to make partial admissions of sexual activity. Talking about nonsexual topics that are possibly related to the abuse may be a good ice breaker (i.e., photography, collection of child development books, etc.). During this period it is better not to use judgmental terms in discussing the abuse. Terms such as *rape, pornography,* and *molestation* will convey to the suspect the illegality of his actions. Substitute terms that are descriptive of the activity (e.g., "taking

> *Talking about nonsexual topics may be a good ice breaker.*

nude photos," "placing your penis in her mouth"), take some of the sting out of the difficulty in admitting and also clarify exactly what types of sexual interactions are being discussed.

Generally, the offender will begin by minimizing the quality and quantity of the sexual activity in which he has engaged. This is usually the tip of the iceberg. The interviewer who has gotten the suspect to this point can begin to address the improbability of the suspect's position.

In the next step, the suspect usually rationalizes or justifies the behavior. The reasons given might range from providing the child with much needed sex education to doing his own research in child abuse. The interviewer may propose some of these justifications as an interviewing technique. As long as the suspect admits to the behavior, the justifications can be dealt with later.

Some offenders will have done research to find literature that they believe supports their position. A crime scene search might have uncovered this material, and it can be discussed at this time. Under the guise of trying to gain the investigator as an ally, the offender may openly express his feelings on child–adult sexual interaction that can later be used in court. Many offenders run a "trial" justification up the flagpole at this time to determine whether they can convince the interviewer of its plausibility. Some of these have a little truth to them, but many are completely ridiculous. An example would be the man who denied making his 3-year-old have fellatio with him but did admit that, when they were in the bathroom together, his penis "accidentally" fell into her mouth when she turned to ask him a question as he finished urinating. If a suspect is trying to justify the behavior, let him. Again, it does not matter at this point what reasons he gives for the sexual activity. The important thing is the admission to at least some aspects of the behavior. The suspect also is providing the investigator with a glimpse into his mind and the depth of his sexual interest in children. This may be critical as the team makes recommendations to the prosecution, the risk to children is assessed, or the prosecution makes decisions on criminal charges.

It is not uncommon for the suspect to also blame the behavior on others, usually the victim or his spouse or partner: He was under stress, has a drinking problem, was seduced by the child, or in the depths of other life situations that compelled him to engage in these actions that, of course, are atypical of his normal behavior and interaction with children. These are supposed to relieve him of responsibility for his actions. By allowing him to spend time discussing this, the interviewer gets a preview of potential court defenses. The investigator should not be diverted permanently by these tangents and should always bring the questioning back to the primary issues of what happened and all the necessary attendant details before concluding the interview.

Once the admissions are being developed, the interviewer needs to focus on each act in its entirety, as in the child interview. Establishing venue, activity leading up to the act(s), explicit details of the sexual activity, and what happened afterward should be established before moving on to the next act. Moving too rapidly through a series of sexual acts may give an overall view of the extent of the behavior, but it creates difficulty in obtaining enough information to make accurate charging decisions.

When all else fails and the offender realizes that he has been caught and faces serious consequences, investigators might well see what the FBI's Ken Lanning calls the "sick and sympathy" ploy (Lanning, 1992). It is an attempt to divert attention from the victim's plight to the offender's situation. The interviewer (and anyone else who will listen) will hear how his wife will divorce him, his family will disown him, his employer will fire him, and the community will revile him. According to him, he should not go to jail because this "coming out" is punishment enough. His life will never be the same. The community will also hear this sad song should he decide to talk to reporters.

He will be penitent, have learned his lesson, and he will never do this again (read into this, "I will never get caught doing this again"). He may say he needs treatment and ask for recommendations. He will have discovered God and carry a Bible: "God has forgiven me. Why can't you?" Unfortunately, this ploy may be supported by some professionals who will be called to testify on his behalf, as well as by certain segments of the population (who may show up on his jury). If they fall for this, they may minimize the seriousness of the short- and long-term consequences of the abuse to the victim and others directly affected by his sexual molestation. Pressure may well be placed on the victim(s) to forgive him and drop prosecution.

If the suspect is not in custody, discuss the rules of contact with the victim(s). This is of particular interest to the CPS member of the team. In an intrafamily case, will he move out or must the child be placed out of the home? If he agrees to leave, where will he go and for how long? How will he afford it? Does he have any social support systems on which to rely? Will these support systems aid him in facing the situation and dealing with it in a healthy fashion, or will they vehemently support him with his denial no matter what? Child protection professionals will want to know how they can monitor his compliance with this safety plan. The interviewer must also determine whether his alternative plan actually exposes other children to risk (e.g., he plans to move in with his sister and her children and sleep in the children's room). If he is placed in custody, then critical restrictions on victim contact may be included in any bond agreement.

Most investigators feel that the potential for physical danger is low in dealing with child sex offenders, but this is not an absolute. Offenders have tracked down and murdered the victim, hired hit men to assassinate investigators and prosecutors, intimidated witnesses, and even committed suicide during the investigation. Never discount the possibility of violence, particularly if interviews have revealed violence or threats of violence in the offender's past.

The issue of a polygraph being done at some point in the interview process might be considered. For the suspect who continues to deny or vastly minimize, offering him the chance to verify his statement *immediately* can have a powerful impact. For him to refuse to participate looks incriminating, yet if he has not been truthful, he is reasonably sure his misstatements will be detected. The key is in performing the polygraph at that time. Leaving it to the next day will not work: It must be done in conjunction with the interview. In addition, the polygraph examiner needs to be trained in the specific testing of alleged child abusers (Abrams & Abrams, 1993).

If possible, at the end of the interview, the investigator should reinforce the positive aspects of the suspect's admitting to the activity. Stress the negatives of keeping such behavior a secret; praise him for being "man enough" to realize that it is best for all concerned for this to come to light. If the offender has a relationship with the child victim, then point out that with his confirmation of the activity the child might well be spared the ordeal of a trial. Even if the offender is going to be immediately incarcerated, provide him some means of contacting a team member should he want to talk again.

Reinforce the positive aspects of the suspect's admitting to the activity.

The data on female offenders and successful interviewing strategies is extremely limited. Investigators should consult with the mental health consultant or team member to develop case-by-case techniques that would be most effective.

Male juvenile offenders tend to follow the same disclosure patterns of adult males. Interviewers preparing to interview a juvenile suspect need to be aware of different legal obstacles that are in place for this population and revise their interview plan accordingly. In some jurisdictions, it may be necessary to get parental permission to interview the alleged offender, and it is important to remember that juveniles are afforded the same constitutional protections as adults.

10

Validation: The Team Decision-Making Process

All of the team's investigative efforts—interviewing, crime scene searches, medical exams, DNA analyses, lineups, and collateral contacts—are aimed at gathering enough information to make several key decisions.

1. Was this child sexually abused (or subjected to any form of child maltreatment)?
2. If so, can the team determine who was responsible for the abuse?
3. Is the child at clear risk of abuse in the future? If so, from whom?
4. What must be done to protect the child or other children from further abuse?
5. Is there sufficient evidence to support the team's conclusions to meet the standards of (a) juvenile or family court, if needed; or (b) criminal court, if appropriate?

The first two questions are at the heart of the validation process, in which the team weighs the evidence that supports the allegation against evidence that refutes it and, together, team members reach an opinion about what they believe has happened, if anything. Only after doing so must the team consider the other three questions, often allowing the CPS worker to take the lead in the risk assessment process and, with the agency attorney, assess the evidence for juvenile court. Issues of criminal prosecution fall naturally to the lead of law enforcement and prosecution.

Team members must agree on a general criteria for reaching decisions about whether they believe the abuse occurred. This decision often has a specific name in state law, which generally labels such positive findings as *indicated, founded,* or *substantiated.* Negative findings may be called *unfounded* or *unsubstantiated.* If each team member uses a separate and uncoordinated criteria for this decision, then conflicting opinions are likely to emerge for which there will be few productive solutions. Rather, team members should agree on those factors and elements that they believe are important in this most important decision-making process.

An error is devastating. To conclude that a child was abused when, in fact, he or she was not subjects the child to unneeded therapeutic and possible legal interventions. In addition, labeling someone who is guiltless a child molester causes extraordinary hardships on an innocent person. To leave an abused child unprotected may well subject the child to continued abuse along with the despair that would come from hopelessness. Failing to document abuse also exposes other children to abuse. This is frightful when one recalls that many offenders will have scores of victims over decades unless they are detected and stopped. The bottom line is that there is no room for error in a system fraught with human frailty.

An error is devastating.

Against this impossible standard of accuracy the investigative team must decide what elements or combinations of elements in the case under investigation it will consider persuasive. In doing so, team members must realize that in the vast majority of cases there is no scientifically validated method to do so. They also must recognize that virtually any criteria they may choose will be attacked by the defense if the case goes to court. On the other hand, as professionals, they are obligated to use broader professional knowledge and available research to guide the decision-making process.

The validation, as well as the risk assessment process, is not a single event but rather an evolutionary process that emerges over time as the investigation progresses. The team makes some judgment about the information contained in the initial report that influences how rapidly it responds. Certainly after the first interview with the child the team will assess the credibility of the child's statement and form risk judgments about safety. Although the formal decision must await the collection of all available evidence, the team will be constantly assessing the information gathered and acting to stabilize the situation and protect the child.

Currently, there are only two ways to know absolutely that a specific child was sexually abused by a specific perpetrator. First are scientific methods, such as DNA analysis, that establish a connection between the abuse and a specific person through medically obtained evidence. The other virtually certain validation is when the offender has the poor judgment (although this is fortunate for the team) to photograph or videotape himself in the act of abuse. Even in these apparently clear-cut cases, however, attorneys for the offender will attempt either to keep the evidence out of court or to challenge the validity of the evidence.

For the great majority of cases, the evidence will be far less persuasive. In many situations, a team has only the child's statement, some supporting or refuting circumstantial evidence, a statement from the alleged perpetrator, and perhaps some informative but not conclusive physical or medical evidence. At other times all that is available is the statement of a small child. The team's judgment in these cases must be guided by our common knowledge of child sexual abuse and the specific evidence gathered. (See Box 10.1.)

Despite the apparent diversity in types of evidence, most cases come down to the analysis of the child's statement as the central component of validation. In the 1970s, some workers in the field of child sexual abuse said that an investigator should accept a child's allegation of abuse as factual, no matter how general. We were told to "believe the child because children don't lie about abuse." Perhaps this was reasonable advice 20 years ago, before the issue was so

---

Box 10.1: Exploring Evidence

The team should explore the following classes of evidence:

1. the child's statement
2. statements of other witnesses, including other children, nonoffending parents, teachers, other professionals, and other adults
3. medical findings
4. physical evidence
5. behavioral indicators
6. any relevant psychological information involving the child, family, or alleged perpetrator
7. the statement of the alleged perpetrator

---

widely discussed in media and private circles, but today investigators must look far beyond the surface to validate the cases, much less convince a court of the need for protective or criminal action. Competent defense attorneys will explore alternative explanations for the child's actions or statements, so investigators should do this before defense attorneys become involved.

In approaching this issue, the team must begin with an assessment of its own biases and preconceived notions. Despite the obvious capacity for erroneous statements from children, researchers in North Carolina found that 9% of law enforcement officers ($N = 68$) and 30% of CPS workers ($N = 67$) responding to a survey indicated that children "never lie" (Everson, Boat, & Robertson, 1992). On the opposite end of the continuum, the same survey found that 9% of officers and 3% of CPS staff believed that children "frequently lie." Obviously, a strong unsupported bias, one way or the other, can produce errors in decision making.

Experienced professionals who join the team may come with another bias: They may believe that their experience allows them to tell when people are lying to them. However, researchers who have explored this issue have found that samples of probation officers, graduate students, and social workers did no better than chance in determining which children in the study were telling false stories (about physical discipline). Applicants for clinical licensure actually did worse than chance at the same exercise (Dalenburg & O'Neel, 1991). Team members should remember their limits and keep their biases in check.

❑ Mutual Understanding of Dynamics

Any team discussion of understanding the validity of children's statements should begin with a common understanding of the dynamics of sexual abuse. Sexual abuse exists in three dimensions: (a) the mind of the perpetrator, (b) the mind of the victim, and (c) the legal realm. For example, the offender will generally begin to think of the child in a sexualized manner before he actually initiates sexual activity. It is during this period that he may engage the child (Sgroi, 1982), bringing him or her within the perpetrator's sphere of influence. The perpetrator's actions during this period may be designed to make the transition from nonsexual activity to sexual activity. In fact, this period may go on for months or for just a few minutes.

For example, a stepfather selects one stepdaughter with whom to cultivate a special relationship—taking her on special outings, buying her presents, volunteering to put her to bed, and checking on her at night. Although appearing parental in nature, these actions may be designed to set up the sexual activity. At the other extreme, the stranger who stops a 6-year-old boy on the street to ask the child to help him find his lost dog and then tries to get the child in the car also is engaging the child.

Although the offender's action may have a sexual intent from the beginning, the sense of victimization may come for the child as he or she feels confused, frightened, and out of control. The actual victimization may begin before sexual activity is underway or at least before any physical activity occurs that will constitute a chargeable act.

For example, the child who agrees to get in the stranger's car to help him locate a dog may feel panic when he realizes that the man is driving away and will not let him out. In an intrafamilial example, the stepfather may move from fatherly embraces and kisses on the cheek to a "French kiss." Nothing clear enough to charge on, but certainly clear enough to the child as something foreign and inappropriate for the stepfather.

The actual sexual abuse, in a legal sense, occurs when the child is touched in a location and in a way that state or federal law recognize and define as abusive. The legal concept of sexual abuse is also limited by other factors, including the age of the minor, the age of the person initiating the sexual contact, the consensual nature of the contact in some cases ("consensual" sexual activity between two 11-year-olds as opposed to "consensual" sexual contact between an 11-year-old and a 40-year-old), the type of contact, and even the background of the minor. In some states, adults who have sexual relations with adolescents known to be "bawdy" are not committing, in a legal sense, child sexual abuse.

Within the context of these three dimensions the team can seek a mutual understanding of the dynamics. Several authors have written useful analyses of the dynamics when viewed over the life cycle of the abusive interaction. Roland Summit's classic article "The Child Sexual Abuse Accommodation Syndrome," for example, cites five stages through which sexual abuse may pass: (a) secrecy; (b) hopelessness; (c) entrapment and accommodation; (d) delayed, conflicting, and unconvincing disclosure; and (e) retraction (Summit, 1983). In her landmark *Handbook of Clinical Intervention in Child Sexual Abuse* (1982), Sgroi offered five phases that sexual abuse may follow: (a) engagement, (b) sexual interaction, (c) secrecy, (d) disclosure, and (e) suppression. Both models offer investigative teams a framework within which to evaluate a child's statement.

> *The team can seek to understand the dynamics of sexual abuse.*

Also useful is sharing a common concept of the dynamics of each episode of sexual abuse. In this vein, Finkelhor (1984) has offered a useful paradigm that suggests that four distinct yet variable factors must be in place before an individual sexual abuse incident can occur. The perpetrator must (a) have some sexual attraction to children in general, (b) overcome his internal inhibitors, (c) overcome any external inhibitors, and (d) overcome any resistance from the child.

1. Sexual interest: Investigators might look for ways in which the perpetrator increased his sexual arousal before acting, such as the use of pornography or other erotica.

2. Internal inhibitors: Investigators can look for ways in which the offender overcame his internal inhibitors, such as consumption of alcohol before contact, or predisposing circumstances that naturally reduce control of inhibitions, such as stress, depression, isolation, or frustration.

3. External inhibitors: The team can look for ways in which the perpetrator controlled external inhibitors, such as the father who initiated the abuse after the mother started her night job or the scout leader who singled out one child to share his tent at the far end of the camp away from other adults. Again, predisposing circumstances may play a role, such as the sudden lack of external control that comes with a marital separation and the forced intimacy of a father's new one-bedroom apartment.

4. Child's resistance: The team may find the child was told that "all daddies teach their children about sex this way" or, as John Wayne Gacy did, convince boys that they need to have sexual interactions with other boys or men to learn how to interact with girls (Cahill, 1986). The child's resistance also can be reduced by events such as emotional neglect by a parent or sometimes enticements such as access to drugs, pornography, cigarettes, or alcohol.

Besides providing a useful understanding of abusive interactions, Finkelhor's model also helps to guide investigative efforts, as well as subsequent risk assessment and treatment processes.

The disclosure process is a third type of dynamic that the team must understand. Sgroi has suggested that two types of disclosures are encountered—the purposeful and the accidental (Sgroi, 1982). In the former, the child makes the conscious decision to tell of the abuse. Such cases have obvious advantages for investigators because the child is more likely to describe abuse at first contact. As with most aspects of these investigations, even purposeful disclosures may have their negative sides, including the opportunity for other adults to influence the child's account before the team sees the child, or the fact that the motivations to disclose actual abuse may appear as a motive to fabricate.

For example, a child is told to keep the sexual activity a secret or "Daddy will go to jail and Mommy will divorce him." That may be a powerful reason for a 6-year-old to maintain her silence, but at 14 she may choose to disclose the abuse in a moment of anger, assuming that everything Dad said would happen will happen. Unfortunately, the fact that she is an adolescent and wants to hurt her father will make her statement less believable in some eyes.

The accidental disclosure presents another set of issues. This class of disclosure includes such allegations as those involving sexually explicit play on the part of a preschooler, a pregnancy in a very young adolescent, a sexually transmitted disease, the purposeful disclosure of another child victim who names other child victims, or the observation of the adult–child sexual activity, including the interception of child pornography by postal authorities. Because the child has not decided to talk, these cases present a difficult challenge to the team, which may have to interview the child more than once or arrange an extended assessment.

Sorensen and Snow (1991) found that in a study of 116 cases in which perpetrators confessed (80% of the sample), criminal convictions were obtained (14%), or strong medical evidence was present (6%), 72% of the children initially denied that the abuse took place. These children required multiple contacts to disclose, with 96% ultimately moving to active disclosure. Some 74% of the disclosures in the study were accidental. As Summit and Sgroi predicted in their models, this study found that 22% of the children, where we know the abuse occurred, actually recanted their disclosure at some point in the investigation (with 92% reaffirming their initial disclosure over time) (Sorensen & Snow, 1991). Understanding this disclosure process is important to team decision making.

❏ Analyzing the Child's Statement

With an understanding of the dynamics of abuse and disclosure, the team will need to decide what factors in the child's statement will be examined and what significance to attach to each one. Many writers have offered suggestions about what to look for in a child's statement, beginning with the work of Sgroi, Porter, and Blick in 1982. At least one state, Tennessee, has incorporated a validation criteria in administrative law. Some of the literature is targeted exclusively at mental health clinicians doing forensic assessments in divorce custody disputes. Some of those who have written on this subject are most closely associated with defense attorneys and often appear as defense experts.

For investigative team purposes, we suggest that the team consider the following:

1. Look for multiple incidents. Most abuse involves multiple incidents over time (Sgroi, 1982; Snow & Sorensen, 1991). *Exceptions:* Multiple incidents would not be expected if the allegation involves an act of opportunity such as a stranger assault at a shopping mall or even an intrafamilial setting that does not allow the offender to often overcome external inhibitors.

2. Progression. When offenders have contact with children, there often is some evolution or progression (Sgroi, 1982) of sexual activity, although it is not the nice linear model some suggested in the early 1980s. Offenders might move from kissing, to fondling, and on to intercourse in a matter of a few minutes or over a period of months. Investigators also often find transitional behaviors (Pence & Wilson, 1992) that allow the perpetrator to bridge the gap between the engagement phase and the sexual interaction phase. *Exceptions:* The team may find some cases in which the perpetrator moved straight to intercourse or fellatio and continues at the same level over time.

3. Details of abuse. This is perhaps the most widely cited factor in analyzing children's statements. The team needs to look for the following:

   a. Explicit knowledge of sexual behavior presumably beyond what would be expected of a child of this age. Sexual detail from a 16-year-old is less persuasive than the same level of detail from a 5-year-old. Focus on sensory detail—what the child saw, smelled, tasted, and felt. Look for experiential detail from the participant's perspective. *Exceptions:* Some children who feel dramatic shame or embarrassment will provide less detail. This is particularly true of boys abused by adult males (Faller, 1988); they are confronting homophobic emotions that sometimes result from same-gender sexual abuse. Also, children who are profoundly traumatized may disassociate from the incident, describing it almost like an observer.

   b. Richness of details and idiosyncratic details. Look for details that give context to the account. Elicit facts such as what the offender did before, during, and after the incident or what he or she said to the child. Ask what the child was listening to during the incident. The team is looking for (a) details that place the abuse in a logical context, (b) facts that can be confirmed (such as the location where the offender keeps his condoms), and (c) idiosyncratic events, or those seemingly unrelated details that the child offers such as talking about the sound of the ice cream truck outside the house during the incident. These are important because they have no useful place in a confabulated story but are consistent with how the mind records actual events (Hoorwitz, 1992). *Exceptions:* Younger children are less likely to provide contextual details (Faller, 1988). Some abusers will engage in activities that provide few if any significant confirmable facts.

c. Internal logic, consistency, and feasibility. Although reports of abuse often emerge over time, starting with denial, then moving to partial disclosure, and maybe on to full disclosure—a process equated to peeling an onion (MacFarlane & Waterman, 1985)— often there is a form of internal consistency to children's statements. This takes the form of redundancy of detail (Hoorwitz, 1992). Some core information reappears in different statements mixed with new or more detailed information. Also, the investigator must assess the logic of what is reported. Could what is described by the child have occurred? When logic conflicts with the child's account, the team must consider alternative explanations, such as the capacity of small children to mix fact with illusion established by adults. Sometimes, despite a clear statement from the child, the logical limitations rule out validation, such as the case in which an adolescent foster child alleged that her female caseworker lifted her sweater, loosened her bra, sucked her breast, and then returned her clothes to their original condition while riding the elevator in the county building from the first floor to the third floor without stopping—a ride that takes less than 10 seconds to complete if no one on the second floor stops the elevator. *Exceptions:* The issue of consistency is one of the most difficult to articulate because the child's statements on the surface can be extremely inconsistent, moving from denial to disclosure and back. Some investigators have speculated that some offenders may actually introduce illogical events into the abuse to make the child's statement incredible if he or she breaks the silence.

4. Secrecy: This is a common element of virtually all sexual abuse. Sexual abuse must occur in secret or someone would intervene. If the abuse is to continue, the offender must maintain secrecy. Often the child is told directly to keep the abuse secret, while other times it is unspoken but understood. *Exception:* Faller (1988) found in her study that not all children were told not to tell.

5. Pressure, coercion, and enticements. Explore any factors that led the child to engage in the abuse (Finkelhor's fourth precondition), ranging from subtle trickery to enticements (such as access to activity that is forbidden when nonoffending parents are around) to physical threats or force. Also, determine what the child believed would happen when the abuse was disclosed; in this way the team can ascertain the use of pressure, coercion, or enticement to maintain the secret. Here a range of factors are revealed, from the subtle (such as "If I told, he said he wouldn't be my friend anymore") to the more blatant ("He said he and Mom would get a divorce, he would go to jail, and me and my sisters would all have to go live in an orphanage" or "It would be all my fault" or "If I told, he said he'd kill my Mom and Dad").

6. Other factors to consider include:

   a. The child's affect during disclosure: What was the child's affect or emotional state when talking about the abuse compared to the child's affect when discussing less emotionally laden material? As a general rule, we would expect the child to be more distressed and emotive (emotional) when talking about traumatic events and recollections. *Exception:* Boys are less likely to display emotion (Faller, 1988), and the team may find that children subjected to profoundly abusive environments may have disassociated from the events and present information with a flat affect.

   b. Developmentally appropriate language and sentence structure: Did the child use language consistent with his or her developmental level such as "He stuck his pee-pee in my front bottom and it hurt" for a 5-year-old as opposed to "He had intercourse with me." With all language, the team needs to be sure the child means the same thing as the interviewer thinks it means, such as the child who said "He sexed me," meaning the perpetrator kissed her. *Exception:* Some children are taught the correct names for body parts, and their use must not be automatically be considered a sign of a false report. Rather, if the child uses less mature labels when identifying body parts on anatomical dolls but adult terminology when giving an oral description, it should be a red flag for the team. Also, age-incongruent language also may be present if the child's experience has been interpreted back to the child by other adults before the report to the team. In such cases, the team will have to sort out what is experience and what is someone's interpretation.

   c. Spontaneity of disclosure: Most children are not anxious to discuss traumatic events and require skillful preparation by the interviewer to introduce the subject. Children who appear at the interview with a burning need to tell the interviewer about the alleged abuse without any prompting may be trying to remember what they have been told to tell the team rather than what actually happened. *Exceptions:* Children who have been abused and praised by the person to whom they initially disclosed may have been reinforced for telling and may be anxious to repeat the behavior that won praise previously. Another exception would be an older child who has made the decision to tell of actual abuse and understands the role of the investigator and sees no need to delay discussion of the abuse.

In analyzing the child's statement, the team should consider these factors. It is important that the team weigh all available data. Neither the presence of one factor nor the absence of another should unduly influence the decision. Faller examined children's statements in 103 cases in which offenders admitted to abuse against three dimensions: the context of the abuse, the description of the abuse, and the children's emotional states at disclosure. She found that a majority of the statements (68%) had all three dimensions present, although 15.5% had two, 10.7% had one, and 5.8% of the statements did not fit expectations at all. Factors such as age (young children give less complete statements) and gender (boys give less accurate accounts of abuse details and show less emotion at disclosure) were significant (Faller, 1988). One interesting footnote to this study was that the average age of the females whose statements did not meet any of the three dimensions was 1.5 years of age, while the average age of the males who did not fit at all was 12.3 years. Obviously, these boys could have described the abuse clearly but chose not to. In fact, preadolescent and early adolescent males often have a strong motivation, born of their socialization and resulting homophobia, to deny sexual contact with other males, especially if the contact was coerced.

> *It is important that the team weigh all available data.*

❑ Medical Findings

The presence of medical evidence is one of the most widely accepted indicators of abuse by professionals in the field (Conte, Sorenson,

Fogarty, & Rosa, 1991). Some medical indicators such as sexually transmitted diseases, pregnancy, or the presence of semen in a body cavity are conclusive evidence of sexual contact and, when combined with the child's age or statement, can be a powerful validator. Such evidence, however, is often lacking. Some common forms of sexual abuse such as fondling and oral contact generally do not leave physical injury. Even invasive sexual contact frequently does not leave conclusive medical findings.

❑ Statements of Witnesses

The team will want to consider any information provided by others, especially any witnesses who are reasonably objective and reliable. Rarely will there be a witness to the actual abuse except perhaps when another child sees the abuse as a covictim if the children share a room. More commonly, witnesses are useful in establishing opportunity and history of the relationships, or in reporting what the child or adults allegedly said about the abuse. They may also establish an alibi for the alleged perpetrator or provide a history of prior victimization in the child's life. As with any witness of hearsay evidence, the team must assess their reliability.

❑ Physical Evidence

The team will also consider any physical evidence seized as part of the crime scene. This could include conclusive evidence such as homemade pornography involving the offender and the child or evidence that strongly supports the validation such as condoms and a dildo seized from a drawer where the child said the offender removed them before the assault. Sometimes corroborating information can include such simple things as the child's ability to describe the interior of a bedroom where the perpetrator says the child has never been.

❏ Behavioral Indicators

Many writers who have suggested validation criteria have included behavioral indicators. For investigative purposes, behavioral indicators are useful only when used in connection with other factors such as the child's statement. For example, the fact that a child had a sudden change in school performance is of marginal interest until it is learned that the drop in attention and performance came after spring break, which is when the child said the abuse began. In the early 1980s, several behavioral indicators were cited as significant to sexual abuse. Research has demonstrated that many of these same behaviors are found in nonabused populations, so the team must be cautious not to overstate their significance (Wells, McCann, Voris, & Ensign, 1992). The same study did find that some behaviors were more closely related to sexually abused children, including excessive masturbation, advanced sexual knowledge, unusual interest in sexual matters, and sexual aggression.

❏ Statement of the Alleged Perpetrator

The team should also carefully consider any statement offered by the alleged perpetrator. If he or she denies the abuse, the team must assess any information provided, including possible alternative explanations for the reported behavior (i.e., the foster father who explains he did hug the newly placed foster child but that she thought he was trying to molest her), any motivation the child has to fabricate the report (the child care professional who reported the adolescent's abuse of another child the day before the adolescent in turn alleged that the reporter abused him), or any alibi offered. The team must remember that the offender has a vested interest in covering up the abuse and generally has better cognitive and language skills than the child. In particular, educated offenders can present a convincing denial and when dealing with them, the team must not be dissuaded by their sophistication. Some offenders will make partial admissions, admitting one incident or an attempt.

Well-functioning teams report a high rate of full admissions, and such statements obviously will play a definitive role in the team's decision making. Under this category, the team would also assess any surreptitiously recorded statements of the suspect.

❏ Pulling It All Together

Each factor must be weighed along with any other relevant information gathered by the team. The team must remember that there is no scientifically validated way to determine the validity of all sexual abuse cases. Sometimes it will be clear that the abuse occurred and who is responsible. At other times the team will be confident that the abuse did not occur. Unfortunately, most cases are not that simple. Often the team will need to consider all data, drawing conclusions from the constellation of factors that, when considered together, will lead the team to validate the allegation or decide that insufficient evidence exists to do so. If the team believes that the abuse may have occurred but lacks adequate evidence to support its impressions, then a decision must be made to either close the investigation or resume the evidence-gathering phase.

11

Decision Making in Complex Environments

The dynamics of most sexual abuse allegations challenge even the most experienced investigators, but all too frequently the team will encounter issues that further complicate the investigation and team decision making. The most common of these are allegations that arrive in the context of divorce disputes. In most cases there is little motivation for children or adults to incorrectly allege abuse, but custody disputes provide motivation for false claims of abuse and increase the potential for misinterpretation of parental contact. Another area that presents unique challenges to the decision-making process are allegations coming in substitute care settings such as foster homes. Often in these cases the child's history of past abuse may confound the assessment efforts. The third category to be discussed that can confuse the analysis of the evidence are cases that have ritualistic elements. When such allegations surface, too many investigators go off on a tangent, focusing on the ritual rather than the sexual abuse. Finally, the team may confront large-scale investigations—that is, macro cases—with multiple victims and, perhaps, perpetrators. Such cases require special organizational efforts.

To address these types of allegations, the team must anticipate the complexities and the shift that it must make in its normal protocol and validation process. Complicating factors such as a history of conflict between warring parents locked in a divorce requires the team to adjust its understanding of the dynamics of abuse and how a custody dispute can influence the report and investigation. These complexities also call for adjustments in the questions asked during the investigation and what evidence is sought. With modifications planned early, the team can reach reasonable conclusions and take protective action based on evidence rather than emotion or pressure from outside the team.

❏ Divorce and Custody Cases

The public seems to believe that allegations of sexual abuse are common in divorce litigation. Research by the Association of Family and Conciliation Courts in 1988, however, found that less than 2% of disputed divorces involved allegations of child sexual abuse. Most public CPS agencies and law enforcement agencies do encounter a disproportional number of allegations that either surface in the midst of a divorce or are cast by the alleged offender as a divorce dispute. After all, a counterclaim that the allegation is grounded in the animosity of a divorce rather than the sexual behavior of the offender offers a strong defense. Nationally, it appears that children who are the subject of a dispute over custody in a divorce are six times more likely to be the subject of a sexual abuse report than children in the general population (Thoennes & Tjaden, 1990).

The prevalence of "false" allegations of abuse in these cases has been the topic of some debate. Virtually all of the studies in this area are plagued by methodological problems of sample size, imprecise measures of which cases constitute a false allegation, or both. Most cases rely on the authors' own validation criteria, which are subject to the frailties of human judgment.

Two studies often cited by defense experts found high percentages of "false" allegations. Green reported that 36% of the cases he studied were false claims (Green, 1986). This statistic is less convincing when we realize that the percentage is based on a total sample of 11 children referred to Green by attorneys involved in contested divorce cases. Even Green's judgment as to the validity of the four cases he believed to be false drew strong criticism in a 1987 follow-up to his report (Corwin, Berliner, Goodman, Goodwin, & White, 1987). Another frequently cited study with a high rate of apparently false claims of abuse was conducted by Benedek and Schetky and reported an unfounded allegation rate of 55% (Benedek & Schetky, 1987). This study, too, suffers from the same criticisms, with a total sample of 18 children.

Studies using larger, more general samples have reported lower percentages of false reports. Jones and McGraw reviewed 576 cases in the Denver area and found only 21 cases that researchers believed to be deliberately false. This study attributed nine of these false claims to adults, five to children, and seven to a combination of both an adult and a child (Jones & McGraw, 1987). A later study specifically looking at divorce and custody allegations involving only 18 cases found that 16.5% were believed to be truly false, with one false case attributed to the child and two to adults (McGraw & Smith, 1992). Although the 1988 study was based on a large sample, the decision-making process to determine which cases constitute false reports is still limited in both studies to the researchers' review of the records and their judgment of validation.

Whatever the actual number may be, it is clear the team must be prepared to address the complex issues that arise in these cases. First the team should seek a common understanding of the dynamics of these cases and modify their protocol accordingly. MacFarlane and Waterman (1986) offered a logical structure to understand these issues. They point out that there are rational reasons why actual sexual abuse will be uncovered during a divorce process.

1. Long-standing abuse revealed during divorce or separation: The abuse may have been ongoing for some time, with the child held to silence by the threat of either family disruption or reprisals by the offender. With separation, the threat may no longer have meaning or the child may fear the prospect of living alone with the offender. Alternatively,

the absence of the offender from the home may allow the child to overcome fear and intimidation and disclose the abuse.

2. The avenging parent: Occasionally, investigators may encounter an offender who sexually assaults a child as a way to cause pain for his estranged spouse. Such cases are rare, but they may be occasionally discovered.

3. The incestuous parent: Some parents who have never acted on their sexual impulses in the past may have their internal controls reduced by emotional stress, loneliness, and reduced self-esteem. They may also be more prone to excessive consumption of alcohol or drugs with the resulting reduction in internal controls. The parent's sexual interest in the child may also be enhanced by the parent's loss of age-appropriate sexual outlets, a concept that Finkelhor (1984) has termed *blockage*.

4. Predisposing circumstances: The change in living circumstances and interaction patterns may facilitate abuse. Where once the father never acted on his sexual impulses because his wife was always around, he may find the removal of the external control associated with the separation too much to resist. The new living arrangements also may ease the transition to abusive behavior as the child may "have" to share dad's bed in his new one-bedroom apartment, dramatically reducing external inhibitors.

All of these reasons help to explain why valid abuse complaints can surface in the middle of a divorce. The other scenario investigators will find are those cases in which the child discloses abuse by one parent, usually the father, to the other parent, who acts swiftly to protect the child and separates from her husband. In this case, the allegation is the cause of the divorce, but the offender will usually try to shift the focus to cloud the issue, charging the allegation was motivated by the divorce.

MacFarlane and Waterman also suggested logical reasons for unfounded allegations of abuse to emerge in the midst of a custody case. These include:

1. The avenging parent: Alleged offenders will often suggest that the estranged spouse made up the allegation to retaliate against or punish the accused, but rarely will that be the case. The potential for this approach is facilitated if the accusing parent is emotionally unstable.

2. The overanxious parent: A parent who is depressed and under emotional stress, who may be acutely aware of her former partner's

capacity for physical or sexual violence, and who may herself be a survivor of childhood sexual abuse may be quick to believe that her child was sexually abused during a visit. Such parents may be over-protective and willing to believe the worst with little provocation. A simple parental action during a visit, such as a mishap on a play-ground, can lead one parent to believe that the other has abused the child. For example, if a child falls on the monkey bars while her father was helping her and endures a minor straddle injury, she might report to her mother that her daddy "hurt her pee-pee." With her negative feelings toward the father and concern about his capacity for perverse sexual activity, the mother may assume sexual assault and honestly, if mistakenly, insist that the child was abused when she files a report.

3. Troubled child: Occasionally, the team will encounter a seriously emotionally disturbed child whose anger at one parent results in a false report. A past experience with sexual victimization would fur-ther facilitate such a report.

4. Response reinforcement pattern: In some cases, it is possible that a child has said something sexually suggestive to which his or her parent reacted so strongly that the attention reinforced the behavior, encouraging the child to say it again. This is mixed with adult inter-pretations, and a report is made.

To assess allegations in the context of divorce disputes, the team must adjust the investigative protocol and the validation criteria. Investigatively, it is important for the team to understand the history of the relationship. Despite the suspect's claims, the rela-tionship may have been nonconflictual until the allegation arose. Look for any secondary gain on the part of any party that would serve as a motive to fabricate. Also, look for a history of vindic-tiveness by the parties, as well as factors that could lead to a mis-understanding on the part of the reporter such as mental illness, extreme overprotectiveness, or a disturbed child. The presence of these factors does not invalidate the allegation, but it does need to be considered by the team.

From a validation perspective, the team must apply its criteria very finely. If the team suspects that the parent put the child up to the allegation, then such issues as the details of the abuse, the idiosyn-cratic details, the experiential perspective of the report, the sponta-neity of the discloser, the child's affect, and the developmental appropriateness of the child's words become increasingly important.

The team will also need to consider alternative explanations for the report if there is an enhanced possibility that nonabusive behavior will be misinterpreted as abuse. The objectivity of witnesses in these cases also must be carefully weighed.

❏ Substitute Care Settings

Another type of setting in which allegations arise that frequently present complicating factors are reports in foster care, residential child care agencies, and large child mental health or youth correctional institutions. Here are children or youths with previous sexual victimizations and/or emotional or behavioral disturbances that raise questions about their credibility. As in custody disputes, the team must recognize that there are logical reasons for increased potential for real sexual abuse in such settings, as well as an enhanced potential for erroneous allegations.

The team can expect children in substitute care to be at greater risk of abuse by their caregivers for the following reasons.

1. Premeditated abuser: A job in which an individual has unsupervised contact with children for long periods of time ranging from an 8-hour shift to months as a foster parent would be an ideal opportunity for someone sexually oriented to children. Despite this, the presence of such offenders appears to be rare. But they undoubtedly do exist, and the team may find a career pedophile in a substitute care position.

2. Self-seduced abuser: At the other end of the continuum are individuals who come to this work with the best of intentions, perhaps fulfilling some sort of religious mission to help others. Such individuals may well have provided care for years to scores of children without incident. Then, because of stresses in their own lives, with the concurrent reduction in internal inhibitors and the unique characteristics of a specific child, they find themselves spending more and more time alone with the child. One could speculate that, during the engagement phase in this case, the perpetrator is seducing himself as well as setting the child up. He may be taking this fascination with the child one step at a time, not evaluating where this interaction is going until he crosses the line into sexual activity.

3. Sexualized child: Individuals with limited sexual interest in children and youth may well go through life controlling their interest with clear internal controls mixed with external inhibitors and no easy targets. Then as a caregiver, they may encounter a child with a past history of sexual victimization who has been taught to act in a sexualized manner by her birth family. The perpetrator did not enter caregiving to access children sexually but he engages in thinking errors with this child. He may see the child's sexualized manner as a come-on, and he may dismiss the trauma associated with abuse in this case because the child is already experienced and, in his mind, appears to be willing. Then, when considering the risk associated with his behavior, he may rationalize that no one would believe the child anyway and that his credibility will outmatch any allegation by the child.

There are also logical reasons why the team should anticipate an enhanced potential for inaccurate allegations of abuse arising against substitute caregivers.

1. Avenging parent: Potentially, the team may encounter a parent who will knowingly make a false allegation of abuse aimed at his or her child's caregiver, such as a foster parent or child care worker at a residential agency. The same type of allegation also may be directed toward the child's caseworker or a treatment professional working with the child. Motivation for the report may be to avenge a past report by the caregiver or to compete with the caregiver.
2. Angry child: A child, perhaps with a history of past victimization, may believe that a report of abuse will result in a move to another home or be a good way to avenge some perceived wrong inflicted by the caregiver. This type of child is more likely to be an adolescent and may be emotionally disturbed.
3. Misperceived actions: Children who have been sexually abused in the past conceivably may misperceive the nonabusive actions of their substitute caregivers as abusive, reliving their victimization.

When an allegation of sexual abuse involving a substitute caregiver is made, the team is presented with perplexing problems as well as investigative advantages and potential allies. The team will have to adjust the protocol accordingly. For example, it will need to make an early decision about whether to separate the child from the alleged caregiver. If the allegation is valid, to leave the child under the control of the offender is to invite suppression of the disclosure. When working with birth families, legal restrictions limit early removals, but in substitute care settings the placing agency presumably has the legal authority to do so. The agency, perhaps with the team, will need to weigh the risk of reabuse or suppression against any emotional damage associated with removal. This is obviously not as sensitive an issue if the child has been in the placement a week as it is if the placement has lasted five years.

The problem in residential centers can be handled by taking the employee out of contact with the alleged victim, if the agency agrees. This may mean another assignment or some sort of suspension. State law and due process along with reason may require the team only to suggest such action at the outset of the investigation. The agency should understand that the allegation should be taken seriously but that there is no reason to assume it is valid until the investigation is underway.

The agency operating the program often will be an excellent source of background information on the alleged perpetrator and the child. The official records of the agency generally will be reasonably reliable, but any information offered after the allegation is made must be evaluated for bias. Most such agencies also will be licensed by the state, and the licensing authority will be able to secure information from an uncooperative agency that would require a warrant for the team.

The team will need to decide what the appropriate role for the licensing agency will be in the investigation. In some jurisdictions, they will be invaluable allies. In fact, the team may be composed of law enforcement and licensing personnel because CPS will have no authority in some jurisdictions. In making the decision about sharing information and documenting the investigation, the confidentiality of licensing records must be considered because they are public records in some jurisdictions. The team also may find due process procedures in place before information can be released to the agency approving the foster home or employing the alleged perpetrator. This may introduce new actors and even judicial bodies or administrative hearing officers. The team needs to understand these rules in its jurisdiction and be prepared to use them to serve the protective interests of the child and other children.

In evaluating the evidence gathered in these cases, the team should explore several issues, including the current allegation in comparison to the previous history of the child. How closely does this allegation resemble the early experiences? Are the details of sexual activity different from those previously experienced by the child? Is there any secondary gain to be made by this allegation? What does the child expect to happen now? Is there a history of hostility between the person making the complaint and the alleged perpetrator? If the child has a history of fabrication, how does the level of detail of this allegation compare to past inaccurate statements made by the child? How does the child's emotional or psychological capacity influence the likelihood of this being a fabricated statement? Is it possible or reasonable that the child is describing nonabusive interactions but has misinterpreted them? What do other children and adults familiar with the principals have to say?

Ultimately, the team will have to weigh all of the evidence and make a decision. To be inaccurately alleged to have committed sexual abuse is an occupational hazard for those who work with disturbed children and youths, especially those children with a history of sex abuse. On the other hand, even the most disturbed and unreliable children can be sexually abused and may be singled out for that reason.

> *Even the most disturbed, unreliable children can be sexually abused.*

For example, an allegation made by an angry mentally retarded 14-year-old with a long history of lying, including false sexual abuse claims, was validated by a team, which found that the detail provided in this case went far beyond that offered in any previous lie. Further, other children confirmed details about the opportunity for abuse, and one child, who had not had contact with the victim for more than a month, reported that the victim told her about the abuse six months before the victim told any adult. To believe the allegation was intentionally made by an angry child was to believe that this mentally retarded child conceived this lie, set the stage, told a witness, and then waited six months to spring the trap.

❑ Ritualistic Abuse Allegations

Allegations of ritualistic abuse cases have surfaced with increased frequency in the last 10 years. Few things can complicate a case as swiftly as an assertion of ritualistic behavior on the part of perpetrators. The pitfalls in dealing with this situation are legend.

The first difficulty comes with defining *ritualistic abuse.* For our purposes, it is any form of child maltreatment that is carried out as part of a religious or quasi-religious practice or ceremony. Although it is in vogue in some circles to characterize ritualistic abuse as satanic in nature, the team may be more likely to encounter Christian-based abuse. For our purposes here, we are also drawing a distinction between religious ritual and the rituals of individual psychopaths.

In preparing to investigate this form of abuse, the team should be aware of much of the training offered in this area. What is passing for knowledge, particularly around so-called satanic abuse, is highly speculative. For example, what was offered as a "reasonable theory" for why children would be targeted in satanic rituals in 1983 by the established "experts" in the country was being reported as long-established "fact" just five years later at national training conferences. In an area devoid of careful research until recently, the team should take guidance on nontraditional religions skeptically.

Many of the issues around ritualistic abuse are more relevant to the mental health professional who is providing long-term treatment to the child. For the purposes of the investigation, the dominant priority is to remain focused on the abuse, not the religious practice. The most common mistake made by investigators in these cases is to be drawn into investigating the strange religious activities rather than the crime of child sexual assault. When the team hears of the perpetrator reading passages from the Christian bible before the assault, we do not lose focus on the actual abuse. If the same circumstances existed but the report was that the offender read from a satanic bible, many investigators would go off on a tangent looking into the satanic aspect of the case. It is vital that the team remain focused on its mission—the investigation of sexual assault.

To the extent that the team is interested in the ritualistic aspects of the case, it should be to gather evidence that supports or refutes the allegation. If the child alleges that certain objects were used to commit the abuse, then those items should be sought through proper search and seizure procedures. Many of these cases will involve a single victim and perpetrator, but across the country and in other nations there have been large-scale ritualistic abuse investigations. Because of the unusual details produced by valid ritualistic cases, it is critical that the team be properly staffed and structured as in the macro case section below.

The team will need to anticipate unusual complications in these cases. If the allegation is valid, the levels of secrecy, pressure, and coercion are likely to be extreme. The ritualistic perpetrator can use much more persuasive pressure on the child by invoking supernatural powers to enforce silence. These omnipresent threats, when mixed with real world threats of violence or reprisal, can be powerful. For many ritual abuse victims, the use of extended assessment will be necessary to gain a full disclosure. Avoid using "ritualistic-specific" interviewing aids. Such material used at the investigative stage can taint any information given by the child.

Timely search warrants will be necessary if the team wishes to find and seize corroborating physical evidence. Many ritual cases have required far too long to begin the search process and have come up empty. The delayed and unsuccessful search may actually cause more harm than good because it will be used by the defense at any trial as further evidence of the preposterous nature of the child's claims. If a search is to be done, it must be timely and before evidence is destroyed, altered, or spirited away.

If the abuse is alleged to have occurred over an extended period of time, then the team can expect to encounter victims who exhibit dissociative responses. These children, in their most extreme manifestation, will form multiple personalities. When the investigators meet a child who describes the abuse from a spectator's viewpoint or with a flat affect, consultation with a knowledgeable mental health professional is needed to assess the presence of dissociative disorders. By the same token, if the child talks about witnessing another child's abuse but the team can find no evidence of the other child's existence, then a similar consultation should be sought.

Validation in ritualistic abuse cases comes down to the same process as with others—weighing the totality of all the evidence of abuse. Investigators may find that parts of the allegations can be proven, while others remain unclear or inaccurate. Evidence of the ritual is of value only if it is linked to the abuse. Ritual is not illegal; child abuse is.

❑ Macro Case Investigation: Multiple Victim and Multiple Perpetrator Cases

Most abuse allegations can be investigated effectively by a team composed of a single CPS worker and an individual law enforcement officer working with the prosecutor and mental health professional. In these cases, the team generally must interview no more than a half dozen children and related witnesses. As such, the team can accomplish its goals over several days or weeks. This model, although effective with most cases, is ill-suited to cases involving scores of possible victims, potential multiple perpetrators, or multiple jurisdictions. Such cases are found, among other places, in day care centers; where abuse involves youth leadership opportunities, such as the Boy Scouts; and in pornography and sex rings.

Rather than being a microcosmic example of adult–child sexual interaction, these are *macro* cases: large, global, multifaceted, frequently unwieldy, and extremely frustrating. These cases are the most complex and time-consuming that an investigator is likely to work. The necessity of handling this type of situation correctly from its inception is of utmost importance. To investigate effectively a macro case, preparation and planning are necessary. A team will find it impossible to put into place an effective set of protocols while operating in the middle of a crisis.

There are several major differences between working a macro case and a more traditional case. First, there are the numbers. As noted earlier, the sheer volume of children who are potential victims can be overwhelming. A two-person investigative team can deal with several children as victims, but what happens when there are 25, 50, or 100? Suddenly these investigators, no matter how able, are incapable of meeting the demand. Quickly, there are overwhelmed, burned-out staff wading through reams of reports, unable to advance swiftly through investigative waters. By devoting adequate resources on the front end and dividing the work, investigators can maintain their focus and support one another.

TIME FRAMES AND CASE SIZE

Time frames are different in these cases. The sexual activity may have been going on for decades. This fact alone enhances the investigator's pool of potential witnesses, but it also makes it harder to locate these people. The investigative time frame also changes. In a traditional case the entire investigation, from time of complaint to presentation of the case to the prosecuting attorney in a team staffing, may be only days. Macro cases staffed in traditional ways may consume months of investigator time. Indeed, with only one or two interviewers, just the interview phase may take upward of a year to complete as one child leads to another. The pool of potential victims may grow to such proportions that the investigators may well find themselves dealing with discussions on the "diminishing returns" of continuing the interview process: balancing the need to uncover all persons who are survivors against the realization that with every name that arises a new set of interviews must be conducted and evidence collected and cataloged.

COORDINATION

The need for coordination with macro cases is much greater than with traditional cases. Not only is the usual team challenged to structure itself to accommodate the special needs of the case, but it may also find itself interacting with professional disciplines not ordinarily joined with the team. Macro cases may introduce such actors as the FBI, postal inspectors, customs service, and others. This may also include licensing officials, board of education personnel, private agency staff (i.e., Boy Scouts of America councils, Big Brother/Big Sister, etc.), or a variety of religious officials, all of whom may have a role to play and information to share.

Coordination is needed more in macro cases than in traditional cases.

MEDIA

Media reports on large-scale, out-of-home allegations of sexual abuse often have elevated public concern about investigative procedures, as well as the safety of children in general. This media attention does not stop with the initial reporting of the complaint; it continues as the investigation progresses into the trial stages. The tone of the reporting may shift from calls for aggressive action to suggestions that the team is too zealous. The attention may prompt the unprepared investigator to move more rapidly than the case and caution would warrant. It is critical in the face of such media pressure that investigators proceed methodically and in an organized manner. In the final analysis, when confronted with such a case, the investigative team must pause, plan, prepare, and proceed carefully.

PARENTAL PRESSURE

The most unexpected pitfall of these investigations often has to do with the parents of the children involved. This includes not only the parents of children the team may conclude have been abused but also those of children who are not believed to be victimized but who are connected with the case by virtue of its venue. The mismanagement of the parents may be one of the most common mistakes made in these cases and perhaps even the most damaging to a successful investigation in the long run. Parental reactions may range from complete cooperation to disbelief and obstruction (Pence, 1989). Unfocused parents may engage in activities that are counterproductive to the goals of the investigation and detrimental to the well-being of their children. A system of communication with the parents must be established and maintained. A liaison should be selected to meet, as needed, with the parents to keep them up to date (Interagency Council on Child Abuse and Neglect [ICAN], 1985). Failure to do so may well result in inappropriate sharing of information, frustration with the investigation, and perhaps action that may compromise the investigation and discourage parental cooperation.

Appropriately involved parents can assist the investigation and, indeed, be instrumental in spearheading changes in policy, procedure, or law that may have presented barriers to previous investigations (Hollingsworth, 1986). Involving mental health professionals who can clearly explain to the parents how they can deal with the continuing disclosure process, as well as behavioral manifestations of the abuse, will be invaluable.

LOGISTICAL CONSIDERATION

A more traditional child sexual abuse case involves a minimum of logistical difficulties: a place for the investigators to meet, a location to conduct the child and offender interviews, and a physician to perform medical examinations. All are routine considerations. When dealing with a macro case, the logistical difficulties are multiplied. Where do the normal CPS, law enforcement, or prosecutors' offices find room for simultaneous interviews of 5 or 10 children? How are the children transported safely and quickly to the interview locations? How are medical examinations for 50 children coordinated in a reasonable period of time? This phase of the investigation cannot be underestimated. Just as battles have been lost because the supply line could not be established or maintained, so too can cases collapse for lack of foresight and planning.

Experience has shown it to be more cost-effective to form additional teams and handle the investigative interviews in a relatively short period of time rather than drag out the investigation for months. The additional personnel will usually be needed only for the child interview segment of the investigation. Many law enforcement investigations are now handled in this "saturation" style of investigation, so the concept should not be foreign to enlightened administrators. These additional investigators can come from different sources: Other divisions may have personnel trained in child interviews who have previously been transferred out of child abuse investigations; other law enforcement and child protective services agencies in adjoining jurisdictions may be willing to lend investigators for a prescribed period of time, as is frequently done for undercover narcotics investigations; and state or federal agencies also can potentially assist.

Despite these complicating factors, an investigation can be effectively designed, planned, and implemented to determine accurately the facts and collect adequate evidence to pursue prosecution, if appropriate. The key is planning; devotion of adequate resources, even on an ad hoc basis; and proper execution and documentation. Failure to make the commitment may produce burned-out staff, muddled evidence, and fertile ground for defense experts at any resulting trial.

> The primary objective of the investigation is the protection of child(ren). Investigative personnel have the responsibility to conduct an objective and unbiased investigation and to consider the rights of the victims as well as the rights of the accused. (ICAN, 1988, p. 3)

Another concern of the team is the avoidance of pitfalls that defense attorneys will later use to try to destroy the case. Macro cases defy the public imagination and sometimes even that of the professionals involved in the case. This incredibility factor is easily exploited by those whose primary objectives involve clouding issues rather than determining facts. These people will try to convince the public or jurors that "misguided zealots" (i.e., the investigators) have for some reason fabricated, induced, or brainwashed this preposterous tale into these innocent children's minds. The primary defense strategy that has emerged in many cases is to identify the principal investigators rather than the offenders as the problem. By diverting attention from the defendant, the attorney distracts from the issue of who is on trial and what the issues really are. The defense task then becomes convincing the jury that it is more likely that one or two possibly well-intentioned but inept investigators planted the "story" in the children's minds rather than face the reality of large-scale, methodical abuse of children.

To limit such strategies, investigators are cautioned against relying exclusively on one or two principal investigators and are encouraged to establish two or more investigative teams and even use multiple medical professionals whenever possible. The fewer the professionals, the greater the chance of challenge to individual practice.

In cases in which there are adolescent or adult survivors, the attempt will be made to question their motives for coming forward after years of silence or to challenge the accuracy of their memories. Revenge or animosity toward the accused is also frequently explored as a reason for bringing charges. Although the dynamics are slightly different in dealing with small children, adolescents, and adults, the investigative protocols will be similar.

In day care settings, the need for a well-developed format is critical. In many ways, day care programs are the perfect place for child molesters. They have access to large numbers of children for predictable and extended periods of time. The children are at an age when they are easily controlled by adults, and they are often too young to be effective witnesses against their assailants.

> We can assume the children in these cases are quite young and may have trouble communicating what has happened to them. Young children may not have sufficient vocabulary to describe the incident(s). They may tire easily during the interview, thus making it necessary to have multiple contacts. The assailant(s) has often had considerable influence over the child(ren) and may have had contact with the child(ren) for more waking hours per day than the parent. Investigators also find a greater frequency of female perpetrators in day care cases and a more common link to pornography. (Wilson & Steppe, 1985, p. 4)

INVESTIGATIVE TEAMS AND DESIGN

As soon as the possibility of a macro case arises, the original investigative team should request that additional personnel be assigned. The new investigators should be formed into investigative teams and briefed on the case to date within the limits noted below. These investigative teams should divide into separate units and act as separate cells with absolutely no direct exchange of information among the different cells. The overall investigation and the work of these cells will be coordinated by central team leaders. (See Figure 11.1.)

The macro team also includes one or more prosecutors and access to the appropriate civil attorney if licensing or injunctive action is contemplated. Someone also may be assigned the task of collecting and cataloging the volumes of information. This could be a charting analyst, or one of the coordinators could assume this role.

Each cell will be assigned a cluster of potential victims for interviewing. It is wise to divide the primary cluster or high-risk group of children among the investigative cells (Corwin, 1986). The actual interviewing styles followed are consistent with traditional child interview procedures. Before actual child interviews, investigators

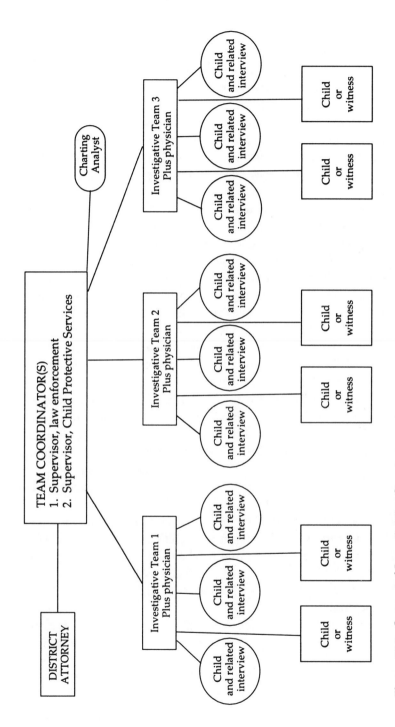

Figure 11.1. Suggested Investigation Structure
SOURCE: Pence (1989).

153

should attempt to ascertain special activities, if any, that have involved the children, such as movies, television shows, games, clowns, magicians, or other similar events. Documenting such events may be important in separating fact from fantasy and in corroborating children's statements. This information may also become critical in avoiding erroneous conclusions that mix actual abuse with a special event in such a way as to mislead investigators to conclude that certain types of abuse may have taken place (C. Cage, personal communication, 1988).

In some macro cases where extraordinary levels of coercion have been used by the perpetrators to enforce the children's silence, or in situations where there are male victims, the children may be particularly slow to reveal what has happened and multiple interviews may be necessary. These children may initially deny all knowledge of the abuse, but then, as they feel more comfortable with the interviewer or after what the child perceives as additional safety controls are in place, they will work through the steps to disclosure: "It may have happened to someone else," "It happened to a friend," "He tried to do it to me," "Something sort of happened to me," "He did a bunch of stuff to me" (MacFarlane, 1985).

The investigative cells also are responsible for all collateral interviews on their children. This includes parents, therapists, other adult witnesses, and physicians. Ideally, a different qualified doctor should be identified to examine the children of each cluster (MacFarlane, 1985; Wilson & Steppe, 1986). The parental interviews may be done either before or after the related child interviews. The team coordinators will usually make the decision on which comes first.

When the cells complete their interviews and prepare their reports, the coordinators will then assign new children to be interviewed. This secondary cluster of children will be those who were identified by the first children interviewed as other possible victims or witnesses, or they may be others whom the coordinators have identified as being at high risk.

The individual investigative cells will not be routinely informed of the results of other cells' interviews as is usually done in traditional cases. In part, this is to counter charges that the investigators were working in concert to pressure the children into making the same statements or that details of the interviews were "cross-germinated" (Humphrey, 1985). It also decreases the likelihood of an interviewer "pushing" the child for specific information known to have been given to another interviewer or misinterpreting something a child says based on information from someone else's interview. It is up to the team coordinators to decide specifically what information is to be shared among the cells.

For example, Team 1 has a child who states that the suspect kept a pair of underwear after a campout. The team coordinators will inform all teams to ask about any articles of clothing that the children might have found missing after a campout.

The team coordinators need to manage all of the investigative data being collected in such a manner as to be able to link evidence to the correct child rapidly. This may be done on a computer or on simple but effective wall charts using large sheets of paper. The sheer volume of work so documented and displayed to the offender may actually intimidate a guilty party into a confession.

Each cell will carefully assess the credibility of what it has been told by the children and other witnesses. The team coordinators, meanwhile, are pulling the big picture together and making judgments about crime scene searches, the coordination of the medical examinations, and ultimately the overall evaluation of the case.

These cases, as complex and initially intimidating as they can seem, can be successfully investigated and prosecuted. The key word is *organization*.

❑ Summary

The team may experience many other complicating factors, from interviews with children with disabilities to children who speak a foreign language not typical of the community. The team needs to be prepared to adjust its protocol and validation process accordingly. The team needs also to be prepared to seek expert consultation when confronted with a variable that is beyond its experience. This will be particularly true when it responds to an allegation in a case involving people with cultural experiences foreign to the team (Heras, 1992). Child sexual abuse presents in so many contexts that the team must be flexible in its approach to the investigation.

When all elements work in concert, the power of the team is greatest.

When all of the elements work in concert, the power of the team maximizes the investigative agencies' ability to determine the facts despite the natural challenges of child sexual assault cases and the unique complicating factors that teams sometimes encounter.

References

Abel, G. G., Becker, J., Mittelman, M., Cunningham-Rathner, J., Rouleau, J. L., & Murphy, W. D. (1987). Self-reported sex crimes on nonincarcerated paraphiliacs. *Journal of Interpersonal Violence, 1,* 3-25.

Abrams, S., & Abrams, J. (1993). *Polygraph testing of the pedophile.* Portland, OR: Ryan Gwinner.

American Humane Association. (1983). *Highlights of official child abuse and neglect reporting.* Denver, CO: Author.

Ards, S., & Harrell, A. (1993). Reporting of child maltreatment: A secondary analysis of the National Incidence Study. *Child Abuse & Neglect, 17*(3), 329-336.

Beitchman, J. H., Zucker, K. J., Hood, J. E., daCosta, G. A., Akman, D., & Cassavia, E. (1992). A review of long-term effects of child sexual abuse. *Child Abuse & Neglect, 1,* 101-118.

Benedek, E., & Schetky, D. (1987). Problems In validating allegations of sexual abuse. Part 2: Clinical evaluation. *Journal of American Academy of Child and Adolescent Psychiatry, 6,* 916-921.

Besharov, D. (1990). *Combating child abuse: Guidelines for cooperation between law enforcement and child protective services.* Washington, DC: American Enterprise Institute.

Braga, L., & Braga, J. (1975). *Learning and growing.* Englewood Cliffs, NJ: Prentice Hall.

Briere, J., & Runtz, M. (1993). Childhood sexual abuse: Long-term implications for psychological assessment. *Journal of Interpersonal Violence, 8,* 312-330.

Cage, R. (1991, November 25). *Guidelines for interviewing child sexual abuse victims.* Presentation to Tennessee Network on Child Advocacy, Nashville, TN.

Cahill, T. (1986). *Buried dreams: Inside the mind of a serial killer*. New York: Bantam.

Ceci, S. J., Toglia, M. P., & Ross, D. F. (1987). *Children's eyewitness memory*. New York: Springer-Verlag.

Child Welfare League of America. (1992). Child abuse and neglect: A tragic trend continues. *Children's Voice, 4,* 8.

Clark, H., & Clark, E. (1977). *Psychology and language*. Orlando, FL: Harcourt Brace Jovanovich.

Colorado Department of Social Services (CDSS). (1991). *Colorado guidelines for cooperation between law enforcement and Child Protective Services*. Denver: Author.

Conte, J., Sorenson, E., Fogarty, L., & Rosa, J. D. (1991). Evaluating children's reports of sexual abuse. *Child Welfare, 67,* 389-401.

Corwin, D. L. (1986, March 11). [Conference presentation]. Invitational Forum on Ritualistic Abuse of Children, Sacramento, CA.

Corwin, D. L., Berliner, L., Goodman, G., Goodwin, J., & White, S. (1987). Child sexual abuse and custody disputes: No easy answers. *Journal of Interpersonal Violence, 2,* 91-105.

Dalenburg, C., & O'Neel, K. A. (1992, January 24). *True and false allegations of physical abuse: Role of the mother in constructing a believable story.* Presentation to the San Diego Conference on Child Maltreatment, Children's Hospital, San Diego, CA.

Deitrich-MacLean, G. (1991). *Protocol for informal assessment of children's abilities to communicate about past experiences.* Knoxville: University of Tennessee, College of Social Work.

Dobrec, A. (1992). An interview with Ken Fields. *APSAC Advisor, 5,* 29-32.

Elbow, A., & Mayfield, A. (1991). Mothers of incest victims: Villains, victims, or protectors? *Families in Society: Journal of Contemporary Human Services,* 78-85.

Everson, M., & Boat, B. (1990). Sexualized doll play among young children: Implications for the use of anatomical dolls in sexual abuse evaluations. *Journal of the American Academy of Child and Adolescent Psychiatry, 29,* 736-742.

Everson, M., Boat, B., & Robertson, K. (1992, January 24). *Beliefs about the frequency of false allegations of child sexual abuse: Where you stand depends upon where you sit.* Presentation to the San Diego Conference on Responding to Child Maltreatment, Children's Hospital, San Diego, CA.

Faller, K. (1988). Criteria for judging the credibility of children's statements about their sexual abuse. *Child Welfare, 5,* 389-401.

Faller, K. (1990). *Understanding child sexual maltreatment*. Newbury Park, CA: Sage.

Faller, K. C. (1992). Can therapy induce false allegations of sexual abuse? *APSAC Advisor, 5,* 3-6.

Finkelhor, D. (1984). *Child sexual abuse: New theory and research*. New York: Free Press.

Finkelhor, D., & Hotaling, G. (1989). *Sexual abuse in a national survey of adult men and women: Prevalence, characteristics and risk factors* (NCCAN Grant No. 90CA1215). Durham: University of New Hampshire, Family Violence Research Program.

Finkelhor, D., Hotaling, G., & Sedlak, A. (1992). The abduction of children by strangers and non-family members. *Journal of Interpersonal Violence, 2,* 226-244.

Goldstein, S. (1987). *The sexual exploitation of children*. New York: Elsevier.

Goodman, G. S., & Aman, C. (1990). Children's use of anatomically detailed dolls to recount an event. *Child Development, 61,* 1859-1871.

Goodman, G., & Clarke-Stewart, A. (1991). Suggestibility in children's testimony: Implications for sexual abuse investigations. In J. Doris (Ed.), *The suggestibility in children's recollections: Implications for eyewitness testimony* (pp. 92-105). Washington, DC: American Psychological Association.

Green, A. (1986). True and false allegations of sexual abuse in child custody disputes. *Journal of the American Academy of Child Psychiatry, 25*, 444-456.

Heras, P. (1992). Cultural considerations in the assessment and treatment of child sexual abuse. *Journal of Child Sexual Abuse, 1*, 119-124.

Herring, J. (1991, October 2). Lecture given at Tennessee State Law Enforcement Academy, Nashville, TN.

Hollingsworth, J. (1986). *Unspeakable acts.* New York: Congdon & Weed.

Home Office. (1992). *Memorandum of good practice on video recorded interviews with child witnesses for criminal proceedings.* London: Author.

Hoorwitz, A. N. (1992). *The clinical detective.* New York: Norton.

Humphrey, H. (1985). *Report on Scott County investigations.* St. Paul, MN: Office of the Attorney General.

Inbau, F., Reid, J., & Buckley, J. P. (1986). *Criminal interrogation and confessions.* Baltimore, MD: Williams & Wilkins.

Interagency Council on Child Abuse and Neglect (ICAN), Los Angeles County. (1988). *Protocol for investigating multiple victim, multiple suspect cases.* Los Angeles: Author.

Jones, D., & McGraw, J. M. (1987). Reliable and fictitious accounts of sexual abuse. *Journal of Interpersonal Violence, 1*, 27-45.

Katzenback, J. R., & Smith, D. K. (1993, March-April). The discipline of teams. *Harvard Business Review*, pp. 111-119.

Krugman, R. (1988). University teaching hospital child protection team. In D. Boss, R. Krugman, M. Lenherr, D. A. Rosenburg, & B. Schmitt (Eds.), *The new child protection team handbook.* New York: Garland.

Landis, J. T. (1956). Experiences of 500 children with adult sexual deviation. *Psychiatric Quarterly Supplement, 30*, 1-109.

Lanning, K. (1982). *Investigation of child sexual abuse.* Quantico, VA: FBI National Academy.

Lanning, K. (1992). *Child molesters: A behavioral analysis.* Washington, DC: National Center for Missing and Exploited Children.

Levine, M., & Martin, D. (1992, May). Drug deals have no boundaries. *Law Enforcement Technology*, pp. 34-37.

MacFarlane, K. (1985, November 10). Conference presentation to 7th National Conference on Child Abuse and Neglect, Chicago, IL.

MacFarlane, K., & Waterman, J. (1986). *Sexual abuse of young children.* New York: Guilford.

Martin, S., & Besharov, D. (1991). *Police and child abuse.* Washington, DC: National Institute of Justice.

McGraw, J. M., & Smith, H. A. (1992). Child sexual abuse allegations amidst divorce and custody proceedings: Refining the validation process. *Journal of Child Sexual Abuse, 1*, 49-62.

Myers, I. (1990). *Introduction to type.* Palo Alto, CA: Consulting Psychologists Press.

Myers, J. (1992). *Legal issues in child abuse and neglect.* Newbury Park, CA: Sage.

National Committee on the Prevention of Child Abuse. (1992). *Current trends in child abuse reporting and fatalities: Results of the 1991 annual fifty-state survey.* Chicago: Author.

Pence, D. (1989). *Macro-case investigations in child sex rings: A behavioral analysis by K. Lanning.* Washington, DC: National Center for Missing and Exploited Children.

Pence, D., & Wilson, C. (1988). CPS and law enforcement: The uneasy alliance. *APSAC Advisor, 3*, 2-6.

Pence, D., & Wilson, C. (1992). *The role of law enforcement in child abuse.* Washington, DC: National Center on Child Abuse and Neglect.

Peters, D. (1991). The influence of stress and accuracy in research on children's testimony. In J. Doris (Ed.), *The influence of stress and arousal on the child witness in the suggestibility of children's recollections* (pp. 60-76). Washington, DC: American Psychological Association.

Roberts, D. (1991). Child protection in the 21st century. *Child Abuse & Neglect, 15* (Suppl. 1), 25-30.

Russell, D. E. H. (1983). The incidence and prevalence of intrafamial and extrafamilial sexual abuse of female children. *Child Abuse & Neglect, 2*, 133-146.

Salter, A. (1988). *Treating child sexual offenders and victims: A practical guide.* Newbury Park, CA: Sage.

Saywitz, K., & Nathanson, R. (1993). *Credibility of child witnesses: The role of communicative competence in children.* Los Angeles: UCLA Department of Psychiatry.

Saywitz, K. J., Goodman, G. S., Nichols, E., & Moran, S. F. (1991). Children's memories of physical examination involving genital touch: Implications for reports of child sexual abuse. *Journal of Consulting and Clinical Psychology, 59*, 682-691.

Sgroi, S. (1982). *Handbook of clinical intervention in child sexual abuse.* Lexington, MA: Lexington Books.

Sheppard, D. (1992). *Study to improve joint law enforcement and child protective service agency investigations of reported child maltreatment.* Washington, DC: Police Foundation.

Sorensen, T., & Snow, B. (1991). How children tell: The process of disclosure in child sexual abuse. *Child Welfare, 1*, 3-13.

Stephenson, C. (1992). Pro: The experience in San Diego. *APSAC Advisor, 2*, 5-8.

Stern, P. (1992). Con: Videotaping interferes with the accurate determination of guilt. *APSAC Advisor, 2*, 5-8.

Steward, M. S., Bussey, K., Goodman, G. S., & Saywitz, K. J. (1993). Implications of developmental research for interviewing children. *Child Abuse & Neglect, 17*, 25-38.

Summit, R. (1983). The child sexual abuse accommodation syndrome. *Child Abuse & Neglect, 7*, 177-193.

Tannen, D. (1990). *You just don't understand: Women and men in conversation.* New York: Ballantine.

Tennessee Network on Child Advocacy. (1990). *Child protective investigative team survey.* Memphis, TN: Child Sexual Abuse Council.

Thoennes, N., & Tjaden, P. (1990). The extent, nature, and validity of sexual abuse allegations in custody disputes. *Child Abuse & Neglect, 14*, 151-163.

Trute, B., Adkins, E., & MacDonald, G. (1992). Professional attitudes regarding the sexual abuse of children: Comparing police, child welfare and community mental health. *Child Abuse & Neglect, 3*, 359-369.

Walker, A. (1992, May 4). *Limping down the road to good communication.* Conference presentation, Kenosha, WI.

Wells, R., McCann, J., Voris, J., & Ensign, J. (1992, January 24). *Parent symptom reports in normal and sexually abused prepubescent females.* Presentation to the San Diego Conference on Child Maltreatment, Children's Hospital, San Diego, CA.

Wilson, C., & Steppe, S. (1986). *Investigating sexual abuse in daycare.* Washington, DC: Child Welfare League of America.

Index

About the Authors

Donna Pence is a Special Agent in Charge with the Tennessee Bureau of Investigation. She currently directs the Bureau's Drug Enforcement Unit. She has been with the bureau since 1976, and prior to that she was a patrol officer with the Nashville Park Patrol. Her assignments with the Bureau have included field investigator, narcotics undercover agent, and child abuse specialist (1985-1994). She has lectured at the local, state, and national levels on investigation of child abuse and child death. she is a member of the FBI National Academy Associates (125th Session), a board member of the American Professional Society on the Abuse of Children, cochair of APSAC's task force on the development guidelines on investigative interviewing of child abuse victims, law enforcement adviser to the National Adolescent Perpetrator Network, a member of the board of the Tennessee Professional Society on the Abuse of Children and the Tennessee Network on Child Advocacy, and a member of the Tennessee Child Sexual Abuse Task Force since 1985.

Charles Wilson, M.S.S.W., is Director of Child Welfare for the Tennessee Department of Human Services. He has worked in public child welfare for more than 21 years. He has authored several articles in professional publications along with a 1985 monograph on child sexual abuse investigations in day care settings, coauthored with Susan Steppe, and the National Center on Child Abuse and Neglect's publication *The Role of Law Enforcement*, coauthored with Donna Pence. He is a past president of the American Professional Society on the Abuse of Children and a past vice president of the National Association of Public Child Welfare Administrators. Together with Donna Pence he is a frequent speaker at national and regional child abuse conferences and symposiums.